Grandchildren
Conferences and Workshops

Yaffa and Shalom Eliezer

Grandchildren
Conferences and Workshops

Authors:
Yaffa and Shalom Eliezer

Published by Booxai
ISBN: 978-965-577-908-0

GRANDCHILDREN

CONFERENCES AND WORKSHOPS

YAFFA AND SHALOM ELIEZER

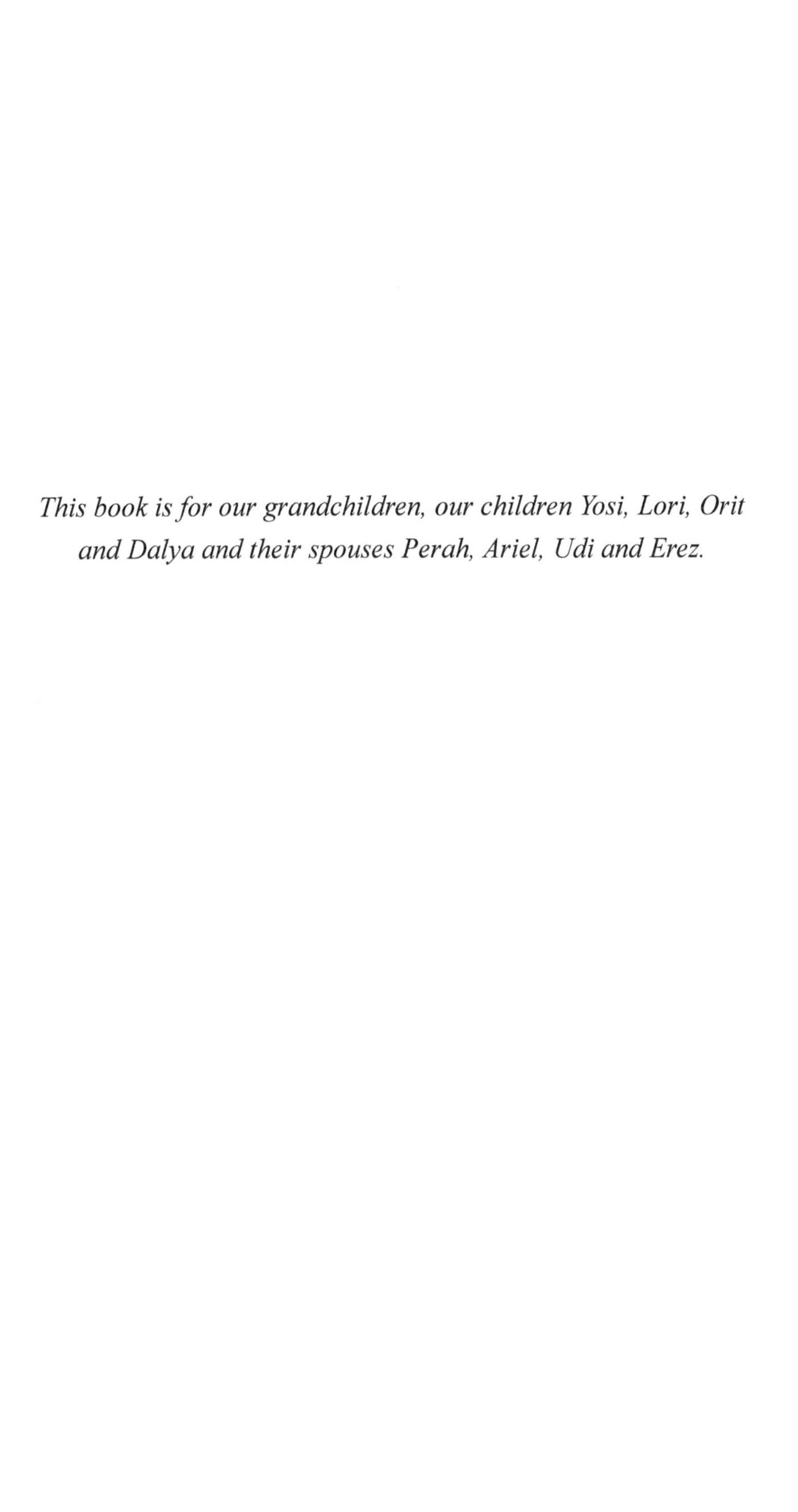

This book is for our grandchildren, our children Yosi, Lori, Orit and Dalya and their spouses Perah, Ariel, Udi and Erez.

CONTENTS

PROLOGUE

November 9, 2019

WE HAVE all come a long way since 2007 and our very first get together. When we first began this tradition of Grandchildren Conferences and Workshops, Gili was not born yet, today Gili, you are in the fifth grade; Alon was a few months old, today Alon, you are in Junior High; Roni and Maya are in their 2nd year of High School; Ori and Eran are in their last year of High School; Shira has graduated from High School and will be enlisting in the army in the Spring; Ido and Tamir are in the army; Dotan and his girlfriend Amit have both finished High School and at the same time have finished their bachelor degree in Physics and are now in the army; and Shani you have finished the army and are now working and studying computer science.

Today, 12 years later, we are at Workshop 10. Most of you

are no longer small children, yet deep in our hearts, no matter how old we are, sometimes we all feel like children.

Saba and I have planned a long and exciting day with some surprises. We tried to prepare a program that could be enjoyed by all. You have always liked to get together and to do projects, help one another, learn together, laugh together. Our motto has always been "having fun while learning". Why did we hold all these conferences and workshops? We did it to hear you say the magic words: "There is nothing better than learning while having fun". I hope today, at Workshop 10, we will continue in this tradition. Let us see what "bits of knowledge" we can take away with us, today.

We have a very busy day ahead including some lectures, films and interesting "personal documentaries". But first we want to revisit all the Conferences and Workshops.

Let us get started.

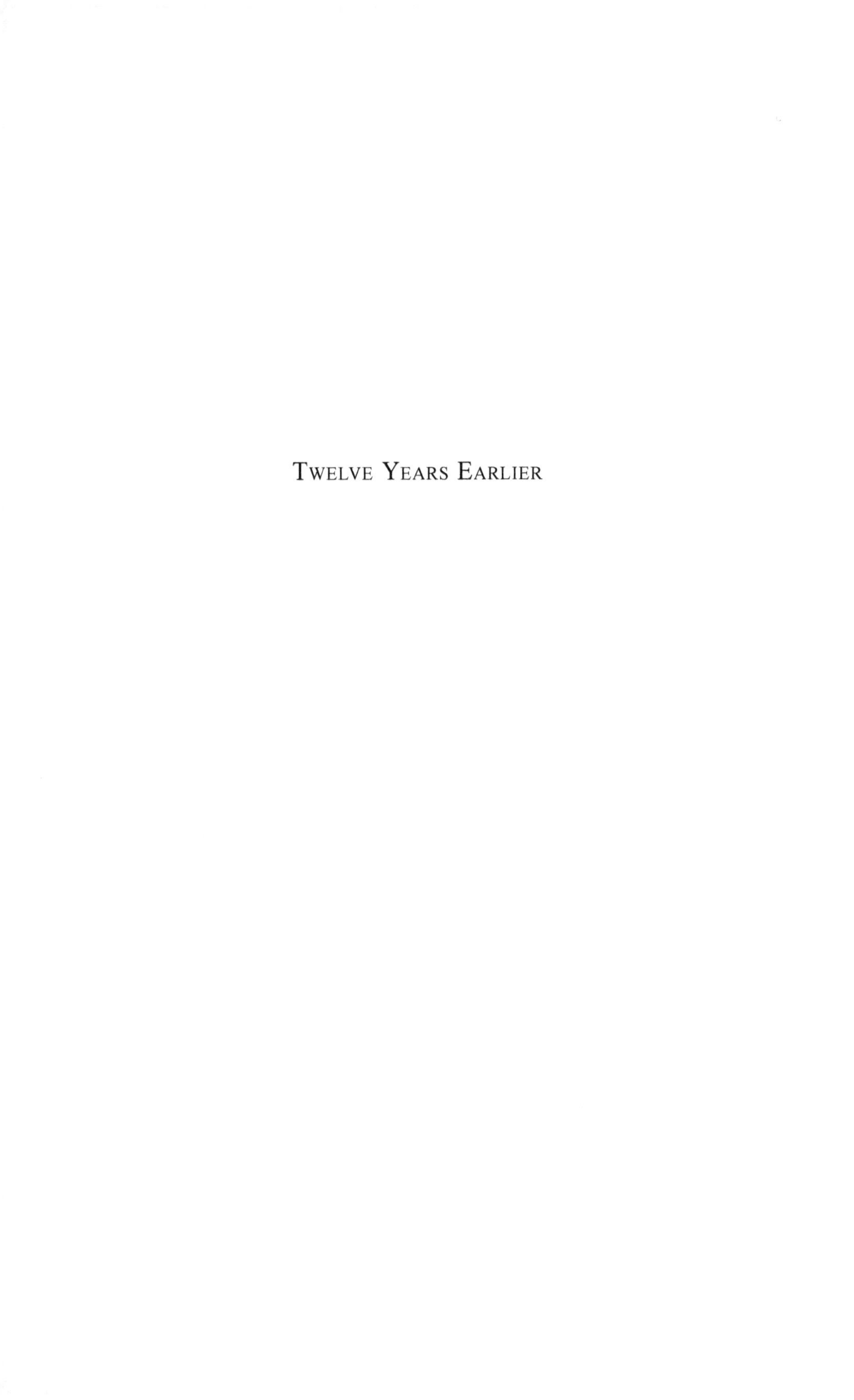

Twelve Years Earlier

CONFERENCE I

GETTING TOGETHER

August 15-16, 2007

The way it all began

SOMETIMES I GET a crazy idea into my head, but once I get started, I just cannot stop. This time I wanted to invite our nine older grandchildren for a sleepover. It would be even better than taking them out because they would be indoors; eat together, sleep together, play together and it would be much easier to keep an eye on them. Simple? Not at all; we are talking about nine youngsters, ages three to nine. At times, it is difficult to babysit only two or three, so imagine all 9 of them together. The truth is that I wanted all the cousins to bond; it was not always feasible. Even if we rented a minibus it would be too difficult to take nine small children anywhere.

Although our four children are in Israel, we do not all live in the same city. We all get together; usually when celebrating a birthday, during holiday dinners or sometimes a Saturday fun supper at our house.

I was so excited that I could not wait to tell Shalom. But as soon as I tell him, he looks at me and thinks that this time I have gone completely insane.

"All of them for a sleepover? Baby Alon too?

"No, just the nine older ones."

I don't think that's a good idea."

"At least let us give it a try. It is only for one night. How difficult could it be?"

"Most of them are still so small. They will scream and fight. What if somebody gets hurt? And how will they all shower?"

"But think how wonderful we'll feel afterwards."

"Think how tired we'll be afterwards."

"So, you agree?"

"I know that if I don't say yes now you won't stop nagging me. I might as well give in and save myself all the arguments."

I could not believe that he agreed! I was so happy and excited. I was sure that the children would be thrilled. But what will we do with them for two days? Suddenly, I begin to have second thoughts? What if one of them really gets hurt; what if one of them wants to go home in the middle of the night; what if it does not turn out the way we planned? But now Shalom refuses to listen to me. He knows that if he does not put his foot down, I will change my mind several times. It was too late; there was no turning back.

Preparations

After looking through my home for art supplies, I prepared a shopping list and made several shopping trips. I bought workbooks, beads, games, etc. The supplies were piling up and the videos tripled because each day I found a better one.

On one of my many shopping sprees, I found a small white board. I knew right away that it was a must. I told Shalom that we would use it for a math corner where he could teach them mathematics. He was thrilled; I had my doubts but for him, the high price was justified. I was sure of one thing; the children would enjoy using the board for other purposes rather than learning math. I was right and wrong.

Besides the endless hours of shopping, I googled for children jokes, short stories and pictures. The paper supply grew low, the toners for the printer dried up and we were off shopping again.

Once I had the essentials at home, I calmed down. I found some old magazines of painters and their paintings and decided to have the children make replicas. This would be something for all of them to do together. What else? Games, movies, stories; my mind was not at rest for one moment.

In between my preparations and cooking, we went shopping again, this time for "the essentials." What did we buy? 9 bath towels, 9 pajamas, 9 water bottles, 9 place mats, 9 scribbling pads, 9 notebooks, and many other things. Among our purchases were also special markers for writing on fabric and plastic and a small "gift" for each participant to take home.

There were not enough hours in the day. Shalom had to take several days off from work to help me with the preparations. We divided the work: I oversaw the program and cooking and he did the labeling for the pajamas and towels and wrote the names on the bottles. It was like sending 9 children off to camp.

Previously

"I'm sorry, I can't come over tomorrow. I received an invitation to the Grandchildren Conference", said the 9-year-old Shani to her friend Amit.

"A Grandchildren Conference! Is it something special?"

"I don't know. I do not even know if my grandparents know. At first my grandmother said that it was a pajama party, then she told me that it would be a sleepover. Now she told me that my grandfather changed the name to Grandchildren Conference."

"Can I come too, please, pretty please?"

"No, it's only for the cousins. I think that one of the reasons that my grandmother came up with the idea is because she wants all the cousins to bond. We don't see some of them often enough."

"Maybe it was your grandfather's idea."

"I don't think so. It's usually my grandmother who comes up with these unusual ideas and then my grandfather improves them."

"What is so unusual about having a sleepover?"

"A sleepover for all nine of us! Sometimes my parents have trouble controlling the three of us."

"Maybe it's different at a Grandchildren Conference."

"I don't know. You know that my grandfather is a physicist and my grandmother has a super imagination, so maybe they are both experimenting with something new."

"Gee I envy you. Make sure that you remember every detail. I will want to hear everything."

"I Promise."

DAY ONE

Our 9 participants Shani 9½, Dotan almost 9, Tamir almost 8, Ido 7½, Shira 6, Ori 5, Eran almost 5, Maya 4½ and Roni 3½.

The big day finally arrived. We even had time to go out for breakfast and relax. At 3:00 p.m. the participants began to arrive. Within minutes they all came; nobody was late that day.

The children were so excited that the noise was incontrollable. This was bad; we had to do something quickly before the neighbors began to complain. I should have prepared a whistle, but instead I called on my vocal cords and surprised even myself at how loud I could shout. This brought them all to attention and the noise subsided.

Before we indulged in the enjoyable refreshments, we went into the kitchen where the children were shown their bottles with their name marked in bold letters. Everyone reached for his or her bottle and swallowed a gulp or two. This already showed cooperation and we were off to a positive start.

Following the water tasting, we gathered around the two tables that were now set up between the living room and the dining room. A light snack of pancakes and vanilla ice cream paved the way to a happy energy-boost.

They were then told to go into the living room to sit down on the small chairs that were set up for them. They pushed each other noisily, trying to grab a seat beside a favorite cousin. We had to "unseat them" and waited for them to be quiet. This time we just sat and faced them and waited for the noise to stop. We finally got their attention and Shalom described the program.

Shalom

Safta (grandmother) and I put a lot of thought on how to do something original and fun with all of you. Safta suggested that we have a pajama party. After several discussions, we decided to call this get-together a Grandchildren Conference. When Eran telephoned to confirm his attendance, he asked me how two adults could take care of nine young children? We know that you will behave, co-operate and help us.

As you can see, we have invested a lot of time with all the preparations. We have set up a few stations of fun. Make sure to visit them all.

Safta has also made some appetizing food that you like, and many sweets. I hope that this will prove to be an enjoyable conference.

Yaffa

Like Saba (grandfather) told you it is important that you visit all the stations. You will receive a small shopping bag which contains a coloring pad, markers, a pencil, an eraser and a sharpener. Before visiting the different stations, take a look at the many nice paintings that we have set up in the dining room. Choose one and try to make a copy in your coloring book.

The stations are:

1. A corner with puzzles and coloring books.
2. One with beads for preparing jewelry
3. Another with beautiful origami paper that we have brought back from Japan.
4. And the big white board; the math corner where Saba is waiting for you eagerly.

We handed them their bags filled with their supplies. They were soon off to the different activities.

The children's reproductions did not resemble the paintings in the art magazines in the least, but they were pleased with their accomplishments.

Both the origami and beads proved very successful; some very nice creations were fashioned. But to my surprise the math corner had the longest queue, and nobody was happier than Shalom.

The three hours passed quickly and by the time it came to wash up, some of them were not eager to leave the stations. With a promise of more to come, they finally agreed to stop.

We knew that wash up time would be the most difficult part of the day. How do you get nine, unwilling youngsters to get washed up quickly? Rewards are always helpful.

This is how the wash up schedule worked:

The two oldest girls were the first upstairs to shower. And behold what a reward awaited them! Each one received a new fluffy towel and a new pajama. Word spread fast and before long everyone was begging to be next. Then the three older boys went upstairs to shower; the four younger participants used the hand held shower in the bathtub downstairs with Shalom's and my help.

Maya and Roni, the two youngest participants, could not stop giggling. What made them get into such hysterics? They laughed at the shower caps that I put on their heads to protect their long hair from getting wet. It took some time for them to stop but finally, they calmed down and agreed to soap each other's back.

At long last they were all clean and dressed in their new pajamas. Shalom and I needed a shower badly, but we could not afford this luxury yet; we had to keep the ball rolling. The two monitors helped set up the table for supper, which consisted of macaroni and cheese, hot chocolate milk and some fruit.

After supper, another surprise awaited them: new toothbrushes, with their individual names, stood ready for use.

Before they could see a movie, they helped us clean up and set up the sleeping quarters which were as follows.

In the living room: a double mattress near the big glass door leading to the balcony, shared by Ido and Tamir.

A single mattress near the piano was set up for Shani; another single mattress across from her for Dotan.

The three other girls, Shira, Maya and Roni, shared the divan in the grandchildren's room. Also, in the room, on the carpet beside the divan, another double mattress was laid out for the two younger boys, Ori and Eran.

Once the sleeping arrangements were finalized, two movies were set up: one upstairs and one downstairs in the grandchildren's room.

Roni, the youngest participant, had trouble falling asleep with the noise from the television in the room and Shalom took her to our bedroom. She fell asleep on my side of the bed.

There were no restrictions for turning in for the night; whoever wanted to stay up and watch television or a movie could do so if he was quiet and did not disturb the other sleepers.

By the time the last participant dozed off it was between 2 and 3 a.m. Shalom had long gone to sleep. As for me, since Roni was fast asleep on my side of the bed, I managed to doze off on the living room couch for quick slumbers, in between my patrols, making sure that everyone was in their place and had not rolled off somewhere else.

Thus, ended the first day of the conference with no major calamities.

DAY TWO

Early the next morning I was the first one up. I rushed into the kitchen for my desperately needed cup of coffee. All was quiet or so it appeared. I barely managed a few swallows before the first early riser began to stir. Too late, he saw me. In no time they were all up and I had to leave my coffee for later.

It was impossible to squeeze everyone around the small kitchen table, so we had to persuade some of them to go into the dining room, which, although much more spacious and comfortable, was less fun with no television.

A breakfast of cereal and hot chocolate milk filled their batteries to battle the day ahead. Once everyone was washed up and dressed, and the mattresses rolled away, no more time was wasted. We began with a variety of games that could be played with two or more players; and continued with origami, making necklaces, drawing, coloring and of course the new board: yesterday for mathematics, today for doodling.

Following the fun with the games, we paired off and Shalom taught everyone the rock and roll with the new steps from our dancing class. This was fun but tiring; everyone was happy when it was time for lunch.

We had schnitzel, rice and corn which was approved by all. For dessert we had a non-dairy ice cream decorated with fruit. This brought on a big smile on each face, including Shalom's.

How good can it get? It gets even better. How about a good

movie? Two were offered again: one upstairs and one downstairs together with popcorn.

At 4 p.m. we assembled once more in the lecture room (the living room) for the closing remarks. We had an exciting discussion; almost everyone wanted to say something. The participants all agreed unanimously that this tradition must be continued.

We then settled around the big table again, this time with home baked chocolate chip cookies and banana cake! Can it get any better? Believe it or not, it can. Following the sweet festivity, each participant received a small bag of surprises. Now they had three shopping bags to take home: one with their new towels and pajamas, one with their water bottles and toothbrushes and one with their artwork and their gifts.

At 5 p.m. the parents began to arrive. The children were excited and showed off their bounty. The parents were pleased that the children had had such a good time, but no one felt happier than Shalom and I. We had made it through the two hard days.

The first conference had turned out to be much more difficult than what we had bargained for. The responsibility and strain of supervising 9 youngsters is a much harder task than we had originally anticipated. Throughout the two days there were ups and downs and moments of "we can't go on". Sometimes the children were noisy. They jumped, screamed and even got into fights. We were constantly "policing" the premises. But courageously we pulled through!

WORKSHOP I

A DAY OF FUN

December 11, 2007

LESS THAN HALF A YEAR FOLLOWING CONFERENCE 1, we convened our Workshop 1 which is like a conference, except that it is a one-day affair.

This Workshop took place during Hanukkah. The reason that the First Workshop followed so soon after the conference was that Shalom and I thought it would be a simple affair. With no sleep over, no mattresses, no showers, no hectic shopping for pajamas and towels, add to that our experience, how difficult could it be? Still very difficult. Although this time we planned a program, we were still dealing with 9 small children, stuck indoors for 8 hours. It was hard to control the noise and sometimes the flying fists. Still, with all the difficulties, at the end of the day we came away smiling. How did we do it?

In general, small children prefer to play, run around and let off steam. As far as they are concerned, they want to have fun when they get together and to leave the schooling for school. So how could we tempt them into a learning mood?

Three things that helped us organize this day: several exploring visits to stores, many discussions and Google. Shalom and I managed to put together an interesting program.

The one-day workshop was from 10 am to 6 pm. The program involved a little more learning and a little less playing. It was the introduction of lectures that paved the way for Conference 2.

On the day of the Workshop, we woke up early and set up the refreshments. Again, we pushed back the furniture; the chairs were brought up from the storage room and set up in rows in the living room; notices were hung in place. Our living room took on the appearance of a conference auditorium and the dining room an inviting working area.

The participants arrived two and three at a time. Soon the house was filled with excitement and chatter. Promptly at 10 we gathered around the table with bottles of chocolate milk and fresh rolls. The children were so happy and excited that it took a while to calm them down. They took the same seats at the table as at the conference so that this was done in an orderly and grown up manner.

Following the refreshments, they went into the living room. This time there was less pushing as each participant took a seat.

Since it was Hanukkah, we decided to take the children back to the days of the Hasmonean period, more than 2000 years ago. Shalom gave the children a short lecture that included a little background material. His lecture was called "Hanukkah Then and Today". Following his small talk, he asked them the following questions concerning electricity, water, communication, and transportation.

Electricity

1. What was used instead of electricity?
2. What did the children and their parents do to pass the time if there was no electricity, no television, no radio or computers?

Water

1. Where did they take water to drink, to wash up or to do laundry?
2. Were there any toilets then?

Transportation

1. What kind of transportation was available?
2. Did the children have bicycles?
3. Did they have horses and carriages?
4. Were there any paved roads?

5. How did a person get from place to place? For instance, for those who had come today from Ramat Gan and Tel Aviv to Rehovot (about 20 kilometers); how much time would it have taken then to come by horse and carriage or on foot?

Communication:

1. How did they communicate with no telephones, no internet?
2. What languages did they speak?

Their replies were very intelligent. They also asked questions; everyone was more than happy to offer their knowledge. It is a shame that we did not record the answers because they were inspiring, full of imagination.

The time allotted for this session was one hour, but it took much longer and turned out more exciting than we had expected.

Next on the agenda was my presentation of a cookie story with a moral value that I had received from my brother-in-law.

A young woman and man were sitting in an airport terminal, waiting to board a plane. They were both eating cookies out of the same bag. The young woman was annoyed each time that the young man put his hand into the bag and took a cookie. She was afraid that he was eating up all her cookies. She had a hard time keeping quiet. Soon the final call was made for boarding. To her great surprise and dismay, she found herself seated beside him on the plane. When she put her hand-case down, she noticed that she was holding a sealed bag of cookies. She realized that he had shared his cookie bag. While she had been angry with him, he had shared his cookies with her with a smile. She felt very ashamed at her selfish behavior and immediately opened her bag of cookies and offered to share them with him. This time when he put his hand inside her cookie bag, she too was smiling.

The cookie story had such an effect on the children that they tackled the next project in a cooperative and friendly manner.

Next on the program, was a competition between the boys and the girls. Each team was given a blank board. The table was covered with different, colorful trinkets (from my many shopping sprees). Each team had to pin as many trinkets as could fit on the board. The boys soon lost interest, but the girls were determined to cover almost every inch of the board. Eran, who had suspected that this would be the outcome, insisted on being on the girl's team. I am sure that you have guessed who the winners were, and nobody was happier than Eran.

This project was followed by a more serious one and called for family cooperation, where siblings worked together.

The projects:

Construction of a castle out of white blocks, using real cement (Shani, Ido, Eran). Construction of two airplanes with guidance from Shalom (one by Tamir and another one by Dotan and Ori).

Jewelry for the young and the young at heart: the preparation of bracelets and necklaces under my guidance and supervision: (Shira, Maya and Roni).

The projects turned out to be a smashing success and the masterpieces were taken home.

Lunch consisted of hamburgers, French fries, corn on the cob and a five in one dessert. What is a five in one dessert? A nice scoop of non-dairy ice cream, some cookie crumbles, fresh fruit, non-dairy whipped cream, and chocolate syrup. This is very tasty if you are not counting calories.

There was a lot of excitement when we set up the card games. The children rotated, trying out different games. Soon the dining room resembled a casino; there was no ringing of falling coins and no exchange of money but lots of enthusiasm and laughter filled the premises instead.

Once the game called "Sets" was brought out, the tension and excitement escalated. It appeared that nobody could beat the six-year-old Shira. The children decided to join forces against her; two, three even four, but still she won. After two games of total defeat they gave up.

The lighting of the 8th and last Hanukah candle for this year was exciting. The first candle was lit by the two oldest participants, Shani and Dotan and then the rest of the candles were lit according to age in ascending order. When all the candles were lit, they all chanted the Hanukah prayers and sang Hanukah songs to the accompaniment of our two young pianists, Shani and Tamir.

Prospects for future meetings were discussed. While I set

up the table for supper for the children and their parents, Shalom continued to have a discussion with the children.

The children wrote, directed, staged, and performed a song and dance routine to thank us for this great day. A few tears escaped my eyes as I watched with pride. And so, the special one-day meeting ended.

CONFERENCE II

ART, STAMPS AND CHESS

July 25-26, 2008

SOME OF MY friends asked me how we came up with the different topics for our various conferences. Besides the hours of thinking, before we decided on the next conference and the right topic, we were sometimes lucky to be in the right place at the right time and not to hesitate to use the opportunity that it offered. In Conference 1 it was the white board that I knew I had to have as soon as I saw it. This board has proved its weight in gold throughout the conferences, workshops and many other occasions when the children came to visit.

My good friend, Edna Gazit, had been on a trip to the Carnival of Venice and upon her return she produced an extraordinary painting of this event. It was at that moment that I knew what the art project at our next conference would be and I asked her for a photo of the painting.

After hours of thinking and discussions, Shalom and I came up with an exciting program with a very tight schedule so that the children would be so busy that they would not have time for any mischief. All went well, except for the unforeseen problem that kept me awake most of the night.

DAY ONE

This year the conference was held in July, much earlier than we had originally planned. Once the date was settled, we had to rush with our shopping. I spent a hectic two weeks buying, cooking and preparing. Shalom took time off work to help me.

At 10 a.m. the children arrived, bringing with them their overnight bags, mattresses, pillows and blankets. This year we were a little wiser and had asked them to bring the bedding from home. There is nothing like experience.

It was so nice to see them so happy together as we gathered around the two tables to partake of our rolls and chocolate milk. Shalom opened the conference.

Shalom

Before I tell you what we have on the program for today, I think that it is time for you to understand why we call our get-togethers conferences and workshops. As you know, I personally have attended many conferences and workshops. I am still going to some of them. In my opinion our meetings "remind me" of these two types of meetings. This is the reason that we chose to call our get together conferences and workshops. We decided that in our case the difference between the two is that a conference is two days with a sleepover while the workshop is a one-day affair.

What is a conference? It is an organized meeting between

people who come to discuss different subjects during a few days. For example, scientists meet on different scientific subjects and present their work or other people's work; this is usually followed by questions and sometimes debates. A workshop is like a conference but there are less lectures because the participants spend most of the time working together, generally in groups.

Asking questions is an important part of a conference or a workshop. These meetings have become so important that besides scientists, other professional groups such as doctors, lawyers, economists, artists and so on organize them too.

As you can see, conferences and workshops are not only for getting together and meeting colleagues and friends from around the globe, but it is a place to learn, to present important new and old ideas in the different professions. These events also include social activities and sometimes special catered food. Safta and I hope that at our conferences and workshops you too will not only have fun but have fun while learning.

Today the subject of our conference is **Art, Stamps and Chess**. Safta and I have planned a full program for you. You will have a painting project, perform a play, prepare an album of paintings. I shall teach you to play chess where we will practice a few moves. We shall look at the stamps, find the name of the country on the globe that issued them; and perhaps even find the subject of art and chess in some of the stamps.

Let's take a look at some of the numbers related to the three topics today:

Art began with the primitive humans about 30,000 years ago. I know that to some of you, this sounds like a huge number and it is. You probably wonder how we know that it began around that time? Because the pictures were found in caves where these primitive humans lived. Today, the scientists can determine the age from the paint. The first modern painting was done in the Middle ages, about 800 years ago, in Florence, Italy by Giotto.

The first stamp was issued on 1 May 1840, 168 years ago in England. This stamp featured the picture of Victoria, the princess, who later became the famous queen of England.

The chess game was invented about 2000 years ago somewhere in the far east of Asia; some claim that it was Persia.

Enough learning of the past. Let us get started with our program for today which includes many surprises from our shopping adventures in Madrid. I will teach you how to play chess and how to start a stamp collection and Safta will oversee the art activities and the adventures that are awaiting you.

Following Shalom's talk, the children were divided into three groups for 3 projects. The first one, under the supervision of Shani, was the preparation of an art scrapbook, composed of a variety of paintings taken from our collection of art magazines. These were the same magazines that were on display in Conference 1. Now they were being used to prepare the album. The pictures were cut out and affixed onto different colored Bristol pages. Shani's assistants were Maya and Ori. Their job was to add some color and make the album more attractive. For this purpose, I had prepared some special coloring books with various designs for them to color with new markers. These pages would be incorporated into the album. Very soon others came to help. They looked like they were having such a good time that everyone wanted "to get in on the action" in their spare time.

The second group with Tamir and Shira as his assistant, was to reproduce on a canvas 70cm×72cm, a replica of my friend Edna's beautiful painting of the Venice Masks Festival from a photo. Here, too, some of the other participants gave a helping hand to complete the masterpiece during the two hectic days.

The third group was to produce a play, based on my short synopsis, using the themes of the conference; art, stamps and chess. Dotan was in charge and with him were Ido, Eran, Tamir and Roni. Rehearsals for the play were done upstairs. The performance would take place on the second day in front of the enthusiastic audience, their grandparents and the other participants.

The three teams worked happily, singing and talking. We were all having such a good time that we did not stop until 1:30 p.m. for lunch.

We were planning to have a big Shabbat dinner in the evening, so we had a quick lunch of Pasta Al Freddo and a special surprise dessert.

Lunch was followed by a two-hour session on one of the most famous Spanish artists, Goya, who is also my favorite. When we told the participants that we were going upstairs, they became excited because they thought that they would be seeing a cartoon or a movie. When they found out that it was going to be a documentary on the artist Goya, their mood immediately changed. But when they heard the word competition, they became happy again.

As soon as the documentary came on, everyone was silent

and put on their concentration caps. When the documentary ended, we went downstairs, and the boys and girls were separated. While the boys stayed in the living room, the girls went into the grandchildren's room and leafed through an art book on Goya that we had purchased in Madrid. Then they had to write down the page number of each painting that they had seen in the documentary. This paper was collected and then the girls switched places with the boys who were given the same assignment. We then went upstairs again to view the documentary one more time. This time the suspense and silence filled the room; the concentration level was at its peak. Everyone was curious to know who had won. You too are probably anxious to know, but you will have to wait until after supper together with the children.

Following the successful Goya affair, everyone was in good spirits and ready to take on the next activity. Shalom and I decided to teach them a dance that we had learned recently at our dance class, the Merengue. Shalom was the instructor and we all formed into pairs. As there were nine participants, I had to be one of the dancers.

Following is the way we were paired off:

Ori and Shira,

Eran and Roni

Tamir and Maya

Dotan and Shani

Ido and Yaffa

The dancing session proved to be much less successful than we had hoped and soon most of the participants returned to the fun stations. The only couples who remained were Dotan and

Shani and Roni and Shira. My dancing partner also deserted me, so I returned to the kitchen to set up the "sweets," fresh fruit. Once our energy levels were elevated, the children returned to the different stations. One thing about time: when you are having fun, it passes quickly and before we knew it, we had to clean up and get ready for Shabbat.

So, who would be the first to wash up this time? Shalom and I developed a raffle system. Nine pieces of paper, each with a number, were crumpled up and placed in a hat. Each child chose a piece of paper and the showers were taken according to the number written on the paper that each child had picked. The older children washed upstairs and the four younger one's downstairs in the bathtub two at a time, boys and girls separately of course.

Washing up was easier this year. The smaller children did not require our help anymore and this was good for our backs. This time the pajamas were a little nicer, the towels a little more expensive and the smiles bigger. Once everyone was attired in their new pajamas, some group pictures were taken; one on the stairs, one on the couch and one in the dining room. These photographs have also become a must in each conference.

The table was set and soon took on the festive look of Shabbat. The four girls joined me in lighting the Shabbat candles; Shalom chanted the Kiddush and everyone partook of the children's wine (grape juice) poured into the disposable goblets that we had especially bought for this occasion. The tasty dinner left us all in a cheerful mood. Even the fact that the boys beat the girls in the Goya completion did not dampen the girls' spirits.

The children helped us set up the sleeping quarters which were the same as the year before except that this time Roni, who was now 4 and a half did not take my side of the bed, but rather shared the divan with her cousin Maya. Shira slept on one of the mattresses on the floor next to the divan. This year Eran and Ori shared a double mattress in the living room, not far from Tamir and Ido. I was tired and looked forward to a few hours of sleep on my bed, but this was not to be.

Once the sleeping quarters were arranged, two movies were set up: one upstairs and one downstairs. The children had so much fun that they had a hard time tearing themselves away. Even the younger ones retired very late. By 2 a.m. I was totally exhausted and happy to be on my bed, but this happiness had a very short duration. I woke up from my deep sleep to the sound coming from the grandchildren's room. Maya was sitting up in bed crying. I quickly picked up the sleeping Roni and placed her on my side of the bed. Then I gently woke up the sleeping Shira and told her to go to sleep on the couch in the living room. I was afraid that Maya's crying would wake everyone. Maya's forehead was hot, and she wanted her mother. Although I had children's medicine to bring down the temperature, Maya insisted that I call her mother. I woke up Shalom and asked him what to do. He told me to call her mother. Maya's mother sounded sleepy but much calmer than I was. She told me to administer the medication and said that she would come in the morning to pick up Maya. After I hung up, Maya refused to take the medication before speaking to her mother to make sure that it was the same medicine and that I knew the exact dosage to give her. What could I do? I called her mother again. After talking to her mother, Maya finally agreed to take the medication. I then applied a damp cloth to her forehead and massaged her back. She continued to cry but this time quietly. It was more than an hour later that she finally fell asleep. I dozed off for two hours or so and when I awoke Maya was hot again. I woke her up and gave her the medication again. This time she took it quietly. I was thankful to see the break of dawn. I do not know why, but it is always much easier to deal with problems during daytime.

Day Two

I had my morning coffee before the first early risers began to invade the kitchen. The children squeezed around the table to have their cereal in front of the TV. I quickly set up the small DVD on the dining room table so that the late risers could have their breakfast too.

Maya woke up much later in the morning. Her mother promised to come to pick her up shortly. In the meantime, she did not want to eat but I managed to convince her to drink something.

Following breakfast, the dishes were cleared, the teeth were brushed, the mattresses were pushed against the wall, the children got dressed and were ready to take on the second day.

A Little Change in the Program

We made changes in the program so that Maya could participate in the stamps venture which was supposed to be in the afternoon. The stamp session was no small affair. Shalom and I had a large stamp collection from our childhood. Some of them were inside stamp albums, others in a box. Shalom's collection was bigger than mine because he continued to collect them from the stamps that were affixed to the envelopes from the correspondence with his colleagues around the globe. He also purchased stamps whenever he went abroad. You would think that we had enough, but when we shopped for stamp albums and magnifying glasses for each participant, we also bought more stamps.

The stamp session was set up in the following manner. First, Shalom gave a 5-minute lecture on the history of stamps. As you learned yesterday the first stamp that became available for purchase was on the 1st of May 1840 in the United Kingdom and featured the face of the young princess Victoria (later the famous queen). Shalom also showed them how to handle the delicate stamps that were removed from the envelopes.

Following his lecture, we placed two huge bowls on the living room table; one was filled with stamps, the other with water. A big globe was placed in the center of the living room table. Each participant received a placemat and a magnifying glass before choosing his stamps. They were then called up one by one, in ascending order from youngest to oldest, to dig into the stamp bowl and select five stamps. These they handed over to Shalom who then read the name of the country and pointed it out on the globe. The stamps were then placed in the bowl with water for a few minutes so that the paper could be removed easily. They were then placed on the place mats to dry.

What stamps were in the pile? Which were the biggest hits? There were stamps from all around the globe; some of them were valuable. But which stamps were the children's favorites? The ones with Elvis Presley, soccer players, the ones from Olympic games and especially stamps from Canada. They also chose stamps from Israel to show their loyalty.

We had hundreds of stamps and the purpose was to distribute them among the participants fairly. When they again dug into the stamp bowl, siblings joined forces to make their choices and cash in on the better stamps before those disappeared. This time they came two and three at a time and after some time the bowl was empty. Before placing their treasures into their Goya bags, purchased in Madrid, the children exchanged some of the stamps with one another. They all promised to place their stamps in the albums at home.

While Maya participated in the stamps project, once this activity was over, her mother took her home because she needed her bed. So now we were left with 8 participants.

By the time we got everything cleared away it was time for lunch. As usual, the stamp project had taken much longer than we had originally planned. I was worried that we were way behind schedule. As soon as we finished eating and had renewed our energies, we continued.

The art album, under Shani's supervision, was completed by now. The children did a wonderful job. Besides the designs from the coloring book, they added their own artistic touches to decorate the album. Tamir and Shira continued with the painting of the masks with help from Shani and Dotan (when they were free). The Drama Group, under Dotan's supervision, rehearsed the play and those who were free played games. One of the big hits was a small soccer game that we had picked up at the Duty-Free Shop. Ori and Eran monopolized this from the start.

The next event on the agenda was "the big" sized games. While on one of my shopping sprees in Madrid, I found three huge games.

1. A chess set with a big mat for the floor to be used as the board and enormous pieces made from durable plastic. To quote Eran when he spoke to his mother on the telephone, "I played with pieces that are almost as big as I am."
2. A game to catch the stick with the rope: five wooden sticks, stuck into a hole marked with distances (20, 30, 50, 60, 100). The children had to throw 5 round loops of cord and catch one of the sticks. The winner was the one with the highest score.
3. A floor matt for the game **X** and **O**. Again, the attraction here was the size.

You must be wondering how we managed to transport these huge games back to Israel within our 20 kilo luggage restrictions. I had to get rid of some of my clothes to make room in the suitcase.

After the huge games were set up, whoever wanted to learn chess learned the first basic moves from Shalom. Soon there was a big line up. The huge chess game had such an impact on Eran, that in the fall following the conference, he joined a Chess group and ever since has become the best player in our group.

And here is something that I spent some time compiling and the children hardly touched; a pamphlet with the history of chess, featuring beautiful pictures of chess pieces throughout the centuries around the globe. The children barely took the time to glance through it. Maybe when they get older, they will find some more interest in it. In the meantime, it will sit and gather dust like some of my other enthusiastic ideas.

We also set up other board games and the children spent an hour of fun. Then we had another surprise waiting; something else that we brought back from Madrid; a monopoly game played with chocolates. In this game, each time that one lands on a property he receives a chocolate; sometimes one, other times two or more, depending on the value of the property. Scrumptious chocolate pieces wrapped in beautiful wrappers.

And then it was time to see all the successful accomplishments of the past two days. The art album was displayed, and everyone took turns looking at the beautiful paintings. Then the painting of the masks was unveiled. It was an amazing reproduction of my friend's original.

When I brought it to the shop to have it framed, the shop owner was amazed that it had been done by such young children. Today, it still hangs proudly in the grandchildren's room together with their other accomplishments. Too bad that we did not use paint instead of the markers which by now have faded somewhat.

For the finale, we all went into the living room to see the third project: the play by the Drama Group, headed by Dotan with Tamir, Ido, Eran and little Roni.

The children did an excellent interpretation of the play. There was very little dialogue but there was a lot of action and they used all the themes that I had requested. They had the scene at the coffee shop where two players had a game of chess and set up the wager; the writing of the letter to Vincent Van Gogh; the purchasing of the stamp; the visit to Van Gogh by horse and carriage; the meeting with Van Gogh and then the final scene at the coffee shop. They received a lot of cheering and applause and had to take several bows before we let them sit down.

Before going home, the children received some nice souvenirs which included a tote bag with a picture of Goya, a cameo of Goya's work, a little notebook with a cover of a well-known painting and some other mementos.

And then the magic moment came. The bell sounded and the parents arrived to pick up their crew. It had been a good conference and it went well but right now Shalom and I wanted peace and quiet.

Something to think about: A week or so later when we saw the four and half-year-old Roni, our youngest participant then, Shalom asked her if she took the Goya cameo to show her nursery teacher. Her reply was "no, I don't think that she knows who Goya is".

For those who are curious, we have decided to include in this Conference the program (before the changes) and the menu:

The Program

Friday

10:00 Around the table for a bite and chocolate milk

10:30 Opening of the Conference and details of the program

11:00 The preparation of an art album
Painting on canvas
The preparation of a play

13:30 Lunch

14:30 A documentary and competition about the famous
Spanish painter Goya

16:30 Time out for a snack

17:00 Arts and Crafts, followed by a dancing lesson

18:30 Showers

19:30 Kiddush for Shabbat
Shabbat dinner

20:30 Two movies; one upstairs, one downstairs

Saturday

8:30 Rise and shine

9:00 Breakfast

10:00 Games

13:00 Lunch

14:00 Stamps

16:00 Snack

16:30 More games, practicing the new dance, completion of the painting.
Exhibiting the new art album, performance of the play, and handing out the gifts to take home.

18:30 Supper

19:30 The parents arrive to pick up the children.

THE MENU

<u>Morning</u>
Chocolate Milk and rolls

<u>Friday lunch</u>
Pasta Alfredo
Surprise dessert

<u>Friday Night Supper</u>
Chicken in the oven, noodle dish, salad, dessert

<u>Saturday breakfast:</u>
Cheerios with milk
Pancakes
Cookies
Fruit

<u>Lunch</u>
Schnitzel, rice, salad, corn, and a surprise dessert

<u>Supper</u>
French toast, a variety of Danish, fruit, and sweets

A Few weeks after

A few weeks after the Conference, at one of my Scribblers Meeting, I wrote a short story based on the themes of Conference 2.

The Wager (Yaffa Eliezer September 2008)

It is 1889, the trees along the tree-lined promenade have lost their leaves, the gas lamps are lit earlier, the pedestrians are bundled up; autumn has arrived in Paris.

In one of the coffee shops on Avenue Champs Elysees, two young men are swallowing their last drops of red wine before beginning a game of chess. One is a boastful, showoff; the other a bashful, quite intellectual. Before the game begins, the latter, whose name is Claude, turns to his opponent Henri.

"What will be the wager?"

"No wager, definitely no wager! I am certain to win this game and I don't want to take advantage of you."

"What if you lose?"

"I have never lost a game before and I don't intend to lose one now."

"Still, I insist on a wager."

"Very well, you can buy me a bottle of champagne." "And if I win?"

"Then," he said raising his arms in disrespect, "you can name your price."

"If I win the game, I want Jean Francois Millet's painting,

The Sower that he painted in 1850. I have heard that it is in your possession."

"It's a deal," he answered with assurance. He was so confident that he would win the game that as far as he was concerned, the wager could be anything.

The bartender took up his place as the referee. The men shook hands to seal the deal and the game began. The onlookers sat still; the silence was only broken by the sound of breathing and an occasional cough; the suspense was high.

The crowd followed the moves with full attention; everyone's eyes were focused on the chess board, except Henri's. He played quickly and confidently; a smile affixed to his face. Claude played more cautiously, and was in total concentration. The minutes ticked away. Then Claude advanced his bishop and confronted his opponent's king; the game was over and in a triumphant voice he called Check Mate. Henri stared at the board; his face turned ashen; the smile vanished.

"I'm sorry," he stuttered, barely able to speak. "I'm afraid that I cannot give you the Millet painting."

"But we had a wager!"

"I know," he stuttered. "You see, the painting is not in my possession."

"You are lying."

"I wish that it were so, but the truth is that I never had the painting."

The referee was aghast.

"A wager is a wager! This is a very serious matter. You must get hold of the painting otherwise I am afraid that I will have to turn you over to the authorities. Is this understood?"

Henri nodded.

"We shall all meet again in one month", said the referee. You will bring the painting and settle your wager in full. Now I want you two to shake hands again."

The two men shook hands and Henri immediately left. He almost ran to his apartment, his head bent low in shame. When he finally reached his quarters, he was glad to be away from the eyes of the spectators. He had disgraced himself completely. What could he do? A wager was a serious matter.

He poured himself a glass of red wine and paced up and down, drink in hand. Suddenly he remembered a painter by the name of Vincent Van Gogh whom he had met a while back. When he tried to see him again, he was told that he had moved to Arles.

He sat down at his desk and wrote a letter to the painter, explaining that he needed a copy of the Millet's painting "The Sower." He reminded him that during their conversation Van Gogh had mentioned how much he admired Millet's work and that he had copied several of his paintings. Henri stressed the importance of the time and hoped that Van Gogh would be able to help him.

The following morning, he set out to see the painter Paul Gaugin, a good friend of Van Gogh. He found him in his apartments working. Henri explained his problem and asked for Van Gogh's new address at Arles. He told him that he had visited Van Gogh at Arles not too long ago and had returned to Paris following a violent rift between the two of them. A few days ago, he learned that Vincent Van Gogh had checked himself in as a voluntary patient at the Saint Remy asylum.

Henri rushed to the post office where he purchased a stamp which had first come into use in England in 1840 and about 10 years later in France. He placed his letter inside an envelope, wrote down the address for the Saint Remy asylum, affixed the stamp and handed the letter to the clerk to be mailed.

Within a week he received a positive reply from Van Gogh. When he got notice that the painting was ready, he set out personally to the asylum to pick it up. He was so pleased with the reproduction that he paid the painter more money than he had requested.

Finally, the big day had arrived. The spectators crowded the coffee shop. Word had spread, and many more appeared on this day to witness the event. The crowd stretched out to the boulevard. The noise inside was deafening and the referee had to raise his hand for silence. Soon the clamor died down and suspense filled the air. The moment had come for the unveiling. The spectators gasped as the referee uncovered the painting. Everyone stared at the canvas and then all eyes turned to Claude for his reaction.

"This is not Millet's 'The Sower'," said Claude in disappointment. "This painting is a fraud. I will not accept it!"

The referee placed the painting on top of the bar and studied it quietly. He looked at it from different angles, admiring the marvelous colors. The sky was illuminated in a bright yellow; the dark fields were distinct; the solitary figure appeared in motion as he went about his work. The referee turned his head to Claude.

"I think that you are making a big mistake, my friend. Look carefully at this painting. It is very similar to the original and yet it is produced in brighter, more lively colors. I think that it is sensational! I am sure that this painter, this Vincent Van Gogh, will someday become well known.

Take this painting and let the wager be settled."

Claude looked again at the painting. This time he saw it through the referee's eyes and a smile broke out on his face. He shook his opponent's hand.

"I accept this painting. The wager is settled. To you, Vincent Van Gogh, I hope that someday you will be as well-known as my favorite painter Jean Francois Millet."

CONFERENCE III

ART, MUSIC, AND PARIS

August 23-24, 2009

Previously

WHILE CONSIDERING the topic for our next Conference, I
suddenly thought that it would be a great idea to take the participants on a trip to Paris. Shalom thinks it is the most beautiful
city in Europe. We have visited the city many times and
although I tend to agree with him, I prefer to go to Rome.

Now that the children were a little older, we could have a
lot of fun teaching them about the city, its sites and some of its
history.

When I told Shalom that I had found the perfect theme for

this year's conference, "A Visit to Paris", he immediately thought that it was a good idea, but he asked me what exactly I had in mind.

"Remember what a great job the children did last year with the play on their own? I thought that I would write a real script for them about a family of 5 going on a trip to Paris. They could learn the parts by heart and then do a performance for their parents."

"Not so fast. Writing a play is a great idea. Learning about Paris is wonderful but to learn the parts by heart in between all our other activities is just a little too much. Most of them are still so young."

"Okay. So, they won't learn their parts by heart. They'll read them."

"That's better. I'll make you a list of the important sites that we have visited."

"Thanks."

On one of my visits to Montreal years ago, to see my mother, sister, her family and other relatives, I was left alone on a rainy day with five small children while my sister, mother and brother in-law were off for the day to buy meat to fill up the freezer. They would be gone for a few hours and I needed a plan to keep the small five children aged 4 to 9 occupied and out of mischief. I told them that if they do something quietly and stay out of trouble, I will prepare a surprise for them. They promised to behave and were as good as their word while I put together a three act play and a song about a family of five.

I still remembered the song because my children liked to

sing it when they were small. As it dealt with a family of five, I decided to write a play that involved a typical Israeli family of five, going to visit the city of Paris for the first time.

DAY ONE

Now we waited anxiously for the children to come. We had set up the tables and put up some decorations. We had bought an easel on one of our shopping sprees and this was now brought up from storage.

The children arrived, excited and loud as usual at 10 a.m. After the goodbyes and hugs, the parents left, and we gathered around the tables to partake of our rolls and chocolate milk.

Shalom opened the conference and explained the program for the next two days. He said that he relied on them to behave properly. He also said that we had some new surprises for them and a rich program that required a little bit of learning in a fun way.

Then I added that for this conference we prepared new projects that if successful, would be used in future conferences.

We began our program with a discussion on art related to the following questions:

1. Where did art begin?
2. Why were there so many paintings of a religious nature?
3. Were there pictures depicting stories in the Bible?
4. Why were the portraits so important many years ago?
5. At what age should you start visiting the museums?
6. Do you think that today people are still interested in

having portraits painted even though there are so
many advanced cameras?

The children's participation was interesting. Some of them knew some answers, others used their imagination and the session went well. This time when I passed around a few art magazines, they looked more carefully at the paintings.

Following this session, they each received a pencil case with a pen, a pencil, an eraser, a sharpener, a colored pencil, a notebook and coloring block. After carefully inspecting their new treasures they put them away.

Next on the program was a new idea: the coloring of a joint puzzle of 36 pieces. The story behind this goes like this. One day during one of my shopping hunts for new ideas, I stopped at an art store where my attention was captured by some puzzles in the display window. I walked into the store and asked the owner about them. He told me that he himself prepared pieces of thin wood according to the requests of his customers. Immediately I was overcome with excitement as an idea began to form in my mind. I told him to prepare 36 pieces of equal size. I was so excited that I almost ran home and was anxious for Shalom to return from work so that I could share the idea with him. He was immediately "infected with my puzzle bug."

The following day I went to pick up the puzzle and although the shopkeeper placed the pieces carefully in a bag, by the time I came home the puzzle pieces were mixed up. We are talking about 36 blank pieces. You would think that this would be simple to reassemble, but it was not. It took Shalom a while, but finally he managed to assemble the pieces. He then numbered the pieces on the back in a matrix notation so that the puzzle would be easier to be assembled.

The pieces were now mixed up and placed in a bag. Each participant received 4 pieces of the puzzle. Everyone could color the piece to their liking. Soon the children were busy making beautiful designs. As soon as one piece was finished, it was put on a tray to dry. They laughed, sang and talked in a pleasant atmosphere.

Once all the pieces were completed, they were put on a tray to dry and we moved on to our next item on the agenda, a documentary about Paris. This brought on some unfavorable complaints but when we mentioned the magic word "competition," the expressions changed. How was the competition carried out? Each child took his notebook and pencil, watched the documentary closely and wrote down as many sites as possible. When the documentary ended, the girls went into the grandchildren's room while the boys remained in the living room. Each selected a leader, and he or she combined all the sites on one page. Then we watched the video again and the children could add more sights; the ones that they had missed the first time. Shalom collected the pages from each team. We told them that the winners would be announced after supper.

Lunch consisted of honey chicken in the oven, rice, corn and a good dessert. Following this scrumptious meal (as the children described it), we listened to some music by Beethoven. Shalom then gave them a short lecture on the composer, his love for music and his admiration for Napoleon. He told them that Beethoven had dedicated his third symphony, Eroica to

Napoleon but then withdrew it when Napoleon crowned himself emperor.

After the short lecture on Beethoven, Shalom gave one on Napoleon. To our surprise, the children sat quietly and listened carefully. I think they were expecting another competition.

Then we had another surprise, the play. Each one received a copy of the play where his individual part was highlighted with a marker in a different color, of course. We made sure that each participant had a part.

As props, we used pieces of Bristol paper where we wrote the name of each character. Then a ribbon was stapled to the Bristol and this prop was worn by the participants. We also made a list of the different sites in Paris that the family visited printed in large and bold fonts and these pages were placed on the easel up front, facing the dining room.

The sites to visit

Eiffel Tower; Louvre Museum; Les Invalides Museum; Opera House; Champs Elysees Avenue; Arc de Triomphe; The River Seine; Galerie Lafayette; Luxembourg Gardens; Versailles Palace; Notre Dame Cathedral; Orsay Museum

The children read their parts and we managed to do two quick rehearsals. By the time we stopped, the children were very tired, but it was time to wash up, pajama photos and supper. This time supper was a simple meal of pizza and ice cream. When they finished eating, we told them that the competition on Paris was a close call, but the girls had won by one point. When they first viewed the documentary, the girls list contained 9 sites and the boys only 5; when they saw it the second time, the girls had a total of 17 and the boys 16.

Following the meal, they brushed their teeth and arranged their sleeping quarters, the same as the year before. The older ones had a choice of two movies: one upstairs and one downstairs. The younger children were exhausted and fell asleep early. Those who stayed up late were very quiet and did not disturb the sleepers; all except me. We live on the 10th floor and I was afraid to leave them alone upstairs, although the door leading to the balcony was locked and I had the keys. Still, I stayed up until the last one came down to sleep.

Day Two

We had some early risers who took the best seats in the kitchen in front of the TV. Soon everyone squeezed around the kitchen table to partake of cereal and hot chocolate milk.

I rushed them through with the washing up. Once they were dressed and the mattresses put away, we did another rehearsal of the play.

After rehearsing for close to two hours, a new surprise awaited them; the bazaar. Everyone loves shopping and buying new things. The children were so excited that it took some time to calm them down. I am sure that you are wondering how I came up with the idea of a bazaar. During one of my many shopping ventures in Madrid, I bought some monopoly money that was sold without the game. I knew that someday I would put it to good use and the moment had finally come.

How did the bazaar work? The children received an equal amount of monopoly money to spend. This would give us an excellent opportunity to get rid of some of the games, videos and other things that were cluttering up the closet. Of course, I soon realized that the things I had were insufficient and we had to buy many more items.

When I told Shalom about the bazaar idea, he was excited and cooperative but when I dragged him shopping for some enticing objects, his enthusiasm dropped. Shalom hates to shop, but there are things that I do not like to buy on my own.

Besides, his valuable input, I need his strong arms to carry the parcels home.

What things did we add to the games and art crafts that we had at home? We bought two new soccer balls, jewelry, a school bag and some other small trinkets. We ended up with too many things to sell and I had to make room in the cupboards for the articles that were not sold. But the bazaar turned out to be a big success and proved educational as well, although the preparations were time consuming. Each article had to have a price tag. Each child had to receive enough money to be able to afford some of the articles. When one or more participants wanted the same object, we held an auction and the highest bidder could then buy it. All this tedious work was prepared by Shalom of course. He did such a good job that there were never any mishaps. And so, the bazaar idea became a must for each conference and some of the workshops.

Following the bazaar, we had some fruit and cookies before we spent an hour and a half rehearsing the play. Afterwards, although they were tired, they agreed to finish off their crafts.

And then it was time to assemble the 36-piece puzzle. Everyone gathered around Shalom. The suspense was big. You could hear the children breathing loudly as the last pieces were put into place. When the puzzle was complete, everyone agreed that it was a very interesting piece of modern art.

Lunch consisted of schnitzel, pasta, salad, and non-dairy ice cream. Following lunch, the children wrote postcards to one another. These were numbered and we held a raffle to see which postcard would go to which participant. All the children received postcards from one of the cousins. Shani was the only one who received her own postcard. She was thrilled because her postcard was special; and it really was. She had managed to capture some interesting facts about the conference and then sketched a flower arrangement around the words.

On my last shopping spree before this conference, I bought some new games: a mini soccer table (much bigger than the one we had bought at the duty free shop that had been such a hit with Ori and Eran during the last conference), a small shuffle board and a mini pool table. These turned out to be big hits in this conference and the ones that followed.

Before we did the final rehearsal of the play, we brought out the big games and the new purchases, and the children spend a happy hour of fun.

Then they changed into the t-shirts that we had bought when we were in Portugal (I know that it would have been better if they had been from Paris). We had the last rehearsal of the play and when the parents arrived, they were asked to take a seat to view the performance.

THE PLAY

Five People in the Family

The mother is an art lover. In Israel she belongs to an art group who visits a different museum once a month. The father is a simple, unsophisticated hard worker. He is a little loud but a good father and spouse. Some childish humor is added so that the children would enjoy performing.

The cast:

Narrator 1, Ido; Narrator 2, Tamir; Narrator 3, Shira; the father, Dotan; the mother, Shani; the son, Eran; the twins, Maya and Roni; the guide at the Opera House, Ori;

Napoleon, Ido; Beethoven, Tamir

The play begins with the song five people in our family. The children are upstairs and with the script in hand, each name highlighted by a different colored marker, they come down the stairs singing the song "Five People in the Family." Up front, on the easel is a list of the sites that they are planning to visit in Paris.

Narrator 1: An average Israeli family of five are in Paris for the first time. We find them in front of the Eiffel Tower.

The father: We are finally here in this big city.

The mother: I have waited so long for this moment!

The son: Me too.

The twins: Us too.

The father: You are making a lot of noise. Here in Paris people behave properly; they don't shout.

The mother: But you are shouting.

The son: But you are shouting.

The twins: But you are shouting.

The mother and the three children cover their lips and say quiet.

The mother: *Looking up at the tall Eiffel Tower.* Wow, what a height? If you think that I am climbing up all those stairs, then I am telling you now. No way!

The children together: Us too.

The father: Don't talk nonsense. There's an elevator inside. Before we go up, I want to tell you a few things about the Eiffel Tower.

He takes out a piece of paper from his pocket and begins to read. "Why do you think that the name of this tower is called Eiffel? I'll tell you why. It is named after the man who designed it. His name was Gustave Eiffel. This tower was built between the years 1887-1889 for an International exhibition that took place in Paris in 1889 to celebrate 100 years of the French Revolution. More than 100 plans were proposed, but Eiffel's proposal was accepted. The height of the tower is over 300 meters and it is constructed of steel. The width of the base is 5 meters. The tower has a big antenna so that the height reaches 322 meters. It is twice the height of the pyramids in Egypt. The Eiffel Tower was built over a period of two years with only a few workers and not too much money. It was the biggest height of any building in the world until 1930.

Narrator 2: Following their visit to the Eiffel Tower the family arrives to the Louvre Museum.

The father: Remember children quiet. You could follow me, and I will show you the important pictures.

The mother: I think that here you will all follow me. You know that in the art field I am more of an authority.

The son: Mother is in the lead

The twins: Mother is in the lead.

The father: I will make sure that everyone is quiet.

The mother: The names of the artists and their pictures that I will point out are those that I already know.

The first picture, the portrait of a Roman woman, is from the time of the Roman Empire.

And here is a painting by De La Croix who loved to paint historical topics.

He also painted Napoleon on his horse, but that picture is now on display at the museum in Vienna. The French painter Ingress also liked to paint Napoleon.

And here is a painting by Nicolas Poussin who liked to paint religious and mythological paintings as well as landscapes like this one.

Here we have one by the painter Canaletto who was

Italian. This is the painting of the beautiful city of Venice. He painted it so accurately that some experts say that one could know from which building he painted it and from what window. This picture is now here on loan from the Strasbourg Museum.

Here is a painting by the French painter Chardin featuring an average family during 1750.

We finally arrive to Leonardo da Vinci and his Mona Liza.

The son: I know this painting.

The twins: We also know this painting.

The father: Me too!

Narrator 3: I also know who Leonardo da Vinci was and his famous painting of the Mona Lisa. This painting did not always hang here in the Louvre Museum. When Napoleon captured Paris and saw the Mona Lisa, he fell in love with the lovely face and hung the painting in his bedroom so that he could look at her each night before falling asleep.

Now let's join our Israeli family who have just arrived at the entrance of the Dome des Invalides, a large church and the tallest in Paris. The tomb of Napoleon lies here among other French army veterans.

As soon as the family steps inside, Napoleon appears:

Napoleon: I lived in France during the time of the French Revolution. I belonged to the believers of liberty, equality, fraternity. I was born in a house of poverty and I was a plain soldier. Due to my outstanding aptitude and skills at an early age, I was promoted to general. The Age of Revolution was an age of terror. I took hold of power to bestow order and I crowned myself Emperor of France.

I conquered Europe. My name became worldly known. Yes, my name was known all over the world but in the eyes of Beethoven I failed.

First Narrator: Why was Beethoven angry with Napoleon?

Beethoven sits at the piano: I was the most successful composer of my time. At the beginning of my career, I Beethoven, the great composer, had to perform for the rich snobs who didn't understand my music. I played and composed music that captured the whole world.

Oh, how I admired the genius general Napoleon Bonaparte! I even wrote and dedicated my famous symphony "Sinfonia Eroica" in his honor. And then suddenly he crowns himself Emperor. What a nerve? Emperor! As soon as I heard, I erased my dedication.

Third Narrator: After Beethoven leaves Vienna and goes to live in a small village, he suddenly realizes that he is losing his hearing until eventually he becomes completely deaf. Still he continues to compose.

Beethoven's music is one of the best and most famous in the world. Beethoven's music is played even today at the famous Opera House in Paris.

Now, let's peek into the Opera House of Paris. I see our Israeli family is already inside and the guide has just arrived.

The guide: Welcome to the Opera House of Paris. I am your guide and I am pleased to tell you that today we are featuring Verdi's opera "La Traviata".

The son: What is an opera?

The twins: What is an opera?

The guide: Opera is a play that is performed in songs with beautiful costumes, amazing scenery and a full orchestra.

The father: Yes, plays like we have in Rehovot by the children's Drama Group.

The guide: *Angrily!* Opera in Rehovot, there is no opera in

Rehovot! There is opera in Milan, in London, in Vienna, in New York, in Tel Aviv and many more places. Opera is not a play by a youth drama group. The tour is over!

The guide rushes out angrily.

The mother: Why did you mention the youth Drama Group in Rehovot? You and your youth drama group. Since you were a small boy you were involved with the youth Drama Group and now you even registered our children there. We are now in Paris. Why do you have to spoil everything?

The father: You are right. Now we are in Paris.

The son: Now we are in Paris.

The twins: Now we are in Paris.

The father: Quiet, we are in Paris.

Second Narrator: The family stays in Paris for a few more days.

They go to the Champs Elysees, the most famous street in Paris; they visit the Arc de Triomphe; take a boat on the Seine river; do some shopping at Gallery Lafayette

First Narrator: The family walks through the Luxembourg Gardens, go the Notre Dame Church, and Museo d'Orsay that was once a railroad station. This museum houses many famous paintings by the Impressionists and the mother does not want to miss seeing them.

Third Narrator: And finally, the place that the children had been anxiously waiting for Euro-Disney. Am I right?

All the participants shouting. **Yes, yes, yes**

· · ·

Napoleon takes a bow, Beethoven follows, then the family, the three narrators and then the guide from the Opera House. They all join hands and sing the song Five People in the Family.

The end!

CONFERENCE IV

THE IMPRESSIONISTS

July 25-26, 2010

WHEN I THINK about Conference Number 4, the first thing that comes to my mind are the inspiring napkins. It may sound strange, but they played an important role for this conference.

A few months before the conference

We are in Madrid again. My Israeli friend who lives in this beautiful city calls one morning and tells me that there is a very good exhibition of Monet at the Thyssen Museum. When Shalom comes back from work to the Residencia, the well-known residency for visiting scientists and students, I tell him that we must go and see the exhibition.

The following day after an early breakfast, we took the bus to the Thyssen Museum. We arrived early to avoid the many visitors. The exhibition was small, but very enjoyable. After we "washed" our eyes with the beautiful paintings, we stopped at the souvenir shop; a favorite place for buying souvenirs for the grandchildren. This time there were quite a few mementos depicting Monet's colorful paintings. Suddenly, my eyes focused on the beautiful napkins featuring Monet's Waterlilies. I knew then and there that our next conference must be about the Impressionists. When I told Shalom, he was immediately in agreement; even the high price of the napkins did not deter him. We bought 4 packages! Why so many? I promise to explain later. Besides the napkins, we also bought 9 pens, 9 erasers, 9 pencils, 9 folders, 9 notebooks: all with a touch of Monet and 4 beautiful hand watches with a Monet "touch" for our three daughters and our daughter-in-law. We paid and left quickly before I made another "tour of the shop."

And then I remembered something else that made me so happy that I was anxious to return to Israel.

A month before the conference

While Shalom went to work, my days were spent shopping, cooking and in front of the computer searching for material on the Impressionists. The preparations were "full speed ahead".

At one of my stops to my favorite shops for "creative arts," I found some nice, thin, square blocks of wood. I immediately imagined Shalom printing the name of each one of our 9 Impressionists on 4 blocks, leaving enough space for the children to color in each letter so they would feel part of the project in preparing the game. These blocks would be used for a memory game between the boys and the girls. What a fun way to learn and play!

These blocks turned out to be such a big hit that the idea of turning blocks into memory games for different subjects was adopted for some of the following conferences and workshops.

As the date of the conference was nearing, as usual, Shalom took some days off from work. Although Shalom and I were familiar with the Impressionists and had seen many of their exhibitions, we still had to google for information to learn about their personal stories. After selecting our 9 Impressionists, we printed out their images and some of their important paintings from the internet, and then Shalom pasted these onto Bristol paper.

We had a ball getting the premises ready. As we were planning to do some renovations in the house, including having the apartment painted, we covered the walls in the living room with the Impressionists and some of their famous works; the living room was transformed into an art gallery.

Following are our 9 impressionists and one of their famous paintings that we put up on the living room wall for our exhibition:

Edouard Manet (1832-1883), The Luncheon on the Grass, 1863.

Claude Monet (1840-1926), Waterlily Pond, 1899.

Auguste Renoir (1841-1910), Ball at the Moulin de la Galette, 1876.

Camille Pissarro (1831-1903), Apple Picking at Eragnysur-Epte, 1888.

Paul Cezanne (1839-1906), Still Life with Tureen, c.1877.

Edgar Degas (1834-1917), Blue Dancers, c.1899.

Berthe Morisot (1841-1895), Eugene Manet with his Daughter at Bougival, c.1881.

Alfred Sisley (1839-1899), Snow at Louveciennes, 1878.

Frederic Bazille (1841-1870), Family Reunion, 1867.

It was very important for us that the children remember the names of the nine impressionists. To achieve this, we sacrificed our lawn table. We printed out the names of the nine impressionists, many times in different colors. Shalom then cut out the names, glued them onto white paper and these were then glued onto the table. The table was then covered with a transparent tablecloth and stood proudly in the living room, so that the children could get familiarized with the names during the two days.

Why did we buy so many napkins? We spread them on top of the two tables that we used for the conferences (the work area) and covered them with transparent table clothes. We also used the napkins for other decorations because I was left with many, but it is always better to have more than less and imagine if I had run short.

Most of the time I shopped by myself and never returned empty handed. Added to the things that we bought for each conference, such as pajamas, bath towels, hand towels etc., this year we also bought 16 white t-shirts. Why so many? Besides our 9 participants, we also bought a t-shirt for the 4 fathers, for Shalom and two for the younger cousins, Alon and Gili who were still too small to participate.

Also, on the shopping list were green napkins, yellow cups and yellow plates to create an Impressionist atmosphere. We cut up lots of fruit and vegetables for snacking; I bought colorful popsicle trays and prepared popsicles, using fruit juice; all this to add color.

Weeks ago, before I even thought of having a conference on the Impressionists, as I was flicking through the different channels, I saw that one-of them was featuring a three-part BBC documentary about the Impressionists. Shalom and I like their paintings so much that I recorded the series. How lucky can you get? As soon as we came back from Madrid, we watched the series again to make sure that it was "appropriate" for the children.

Finally, we were ready.

Day One

The children began to arrive just a little before 10 a.m. This time the parents took their time leaving. They were so impressed with the decorations that one of them suggested that we hold a parent's conference. Finally, they left, and we were alone with the participants. Before sitting down at the table to partake of our chocolate milk and rolls, something new was adapted and became a must for the conferences and workshop that followed.

Each participant had his photo taken on the lazy boy in the living room. Once all the photos were taken, we gathered around the big table in the hall.

Shalom

Do you believe that today we are going to have our fourth conference? I think that by now our meetings have become unique. I see that you agree with me. As you know our grandchildren conferences are especially designed for you. At times, the subjects are interesting and other times they are less exciting.

Today the conference is about a group of painters known as the Impressionists. You will learn how their movement got started and about their wonderful work that they left behind. As you can see, we spent many hours decorating the premises. We count on you to behave, cooperate, and leave with a good "impression" and knowledge about the Impressionists and their work. There will be many surprises. Safta has worked very hard to produce a play where each participant will have an important role. Before we get started Safta wants to tell you a little bit about the impressionists.

Yaffa

Please come into the living room. Before you sit down, cast your eyes on the beautiful paintings by the Impressionists. Observe the lively colors before you sit down. Look at the round table with the names of the nine Impressionists. Try to visit this table as often as you can so that you can get familiarized with these names. Before you see the first part of a three-part documentary about the Impressionists, produced by the BBC that I had once taped, I would like to tell you a little bit about these 9 famous painters and their backgrounds.

Last year in Conference 3, our Israeli family visited Paris. One of the sights was the Museum d'Orsay where many of the Impressionist's paintings are exhibited. The Museum d'Orsay was constructed between 1898-1900 as a train station but in 1939 the platforms were too short for the long trains and in 1979 the French government turned it into a museum.

Now to get back to our Impressionists, our story begins with Claude Monet who comes to Paris to study with the art teacher Charles Gleyre from Switzerland. There he meets Pierre-Auguste Renoir, Frederic Bazille and Alfred Sisley.

During that time "The Salon", was a prestigious art gallery where all art that was considered important was submitted, but many good paintings were not accepted. Among them was the picture "The Luncheon on the Grass" by Eduard Manet which he tried to exhibit in 1863. Manet decided to use this opportunity and exhibit this and two more of his paintings in the "Salon des Refuses." More people came to see the paintings at the Salon des Refuses than at the "Salon." Monet and his two friends Bazille and Renoir also come; they find the Manet painting that was rejected at the Salon was very good. From this day Monet is very anxious to meet Manet.

Children, look at the wall and you can see Manet's painting, Luncheon on the Grass. It is right below his picture of A Bar at the Folies-Bergere and besides Renoir's Young Girls at the Piano. Today Manet's painting Luncheon on the Grass is considered by many art critics as one of his best achievements.

Now back to our story. Monet and his friends continue to paint with their teacher indoors who complains about Monet's sketches. In the meantime, new colors have been produced in tubes and Monet and his friends finally decide to begin painting outdoors to capture all the great natural colors.

In 1865 Monet is working on his gigantic version Luncheon on the Grass. He wants to try to exhibit it in the Salon, but he realizes that he will never complete it in time. Instead he decides to make another painting "The Woman in the Green Dress," which I am holding in my hand. He uses his mistress Camille as the model whom he later marries. This painting is accepted into the Salon and many people come to see it because they think that it is a painting by Manet. When Manet learns about this painting, he becomes infuriated thinking that someone has used his name. When he learns the truth, Monet and Manet meet up in a Coffee shop and become friends. Manet is a great supporter of Monet and his friends' new style of painting, but he does not adapt this style until much later.

I have spoken for too long. But now I see that I have caught your interest. We are going to see Part 1 of the documentary about the Impressionists. You will learn about how they met, how they became friends, how they formed their group and about their exhibitions.

The children watched very closely the first part and wanted to continue watching the other parts. We promised that they would, later in the program if the time permitted.

Following their good behavior, Shalom read some children's jokes which they always enjoyed.

They then went back to the table where each participant received 4 pieces of the 36-piece puzzle. Inspired by the movie and the many pictures that I was able to accumulate from books, magazines and google, they were to try and capture the Impressionist style. The beautiful Monet napkins of the Water Lilies and the Impressionists' pictures that covered the walls, inspired them to use bright colors. When everyone had finished his last piece of the puzzle, they were all placed on the trays to dry.

After such hard work we needed a snack. That is when I brought out the trays filled with the colorful fruit – green, red, orange, purple and yellow. Then followed the vegetable platter. Everything looked so good that the children managed to eat everything and I was so happy to see them eat these fresh, healthy treats.

We then went into the living room again to see the second

part of the documentary on the Impressionists. How good can it get? Imagine watching the documentary while indulging in popsicle made with fresh fruit juice.

Following the documentary, each one received a copy of the play where his or her part was highlighted with a colored marker. The name of the play was "The Impressionists."

We did a first reading of the play and they were told that from now on until the performance, they had to learn to read their parts well.

The children were tired. We brought out all the big and small games and let them play while Shalom and I and two participants helped set up lunch. We ate slowly and relaxed. For a cool snack after the meal I brought out my experiment: frozen grapes. The children loved them; they looked pretty and were cold; perfect for the hot day.

We were now ready for our next project, the wooden blocks; these were now placed on the table and while Shalom prepared the frame of the names in big, bold letters on each block, the children filled them in with the colors; in each set, 2 blocks, had to be identical. They had a good time coloring in the letters while repeating the names. When all the blocks were done, they were put on a tray to dry.

By now the 36-piece puzzle was dry; everyone gathered around Shalom as he began to assemble the pieces. We were all anxious to see "the masterpiece."

They had done an impressive job! There were lots of greens and reds and yellows and the puzzle was true to its name "an impressionist piece" of art.

Soon it was wash up time. Using our method of the lottery,

adapted in Conference 2, we took the hat and put in nine bits of papers with numbers 1 to 9. In this way showering was carried out in an efficient and friendly manner. Each one received his new towel and pajama and once everyone had washed up, they posed for our pajama pictures; one on the stairway leading to the second floor and one in the living room. Each year, we try to buy the same pajamas for the boys and the same girl pajamas for the girls whenever possible.

Following our enjoyable supper, the children helped clean up and prepare their sleeping quarters. Everyone was in a good mood.

Some of the older participants went upstairs to chat. If they were quiet, we let them stay up; of course, up to a point. The less energetic ones gave in to their sleep demands. When I felt that I could no longer keep my eyes open, I asked them all to go to bed.

DAY TWO

I was up early and even managed a second cup of coffee. Then, slowly, one, by one the participants came into the kitchen; each time another chair was added. They all wanted to eat in front of the TV. When there was no more place to move, the late risers had to take their breakfast into the dining room.

As we had a long schedule ahead, we decided to start the day with the bazaar. Immediately following breakfast, while the children washed up and got dressed, Shalom and I set up the tables. They were always very excited for this event.

This time we decided to have the bazaar in a more orderly way. Once everyone was seated, we brought out the hat and put 9 numbered pieces of paper inside. It was according to this number that each participant came up to see the items that were on sale. After everyone had a chance to view all the items, each one was called, according to his number to carry out the purchase.

So, what was for sale this year: games, videos, jewelry, trinkets, and a few valuable pieces: a backpack for travelling and 2 soccer balls.

The bazaar took much more time than we had set aside; the children were so excited that it was hard to calm them down. Eventually we were able to get their attention with the magic word "competition". We took out the newly designed wooden blocks and played a memory game, the boys against the girls.

The participants gave it all they had, each calling out the name! It was such an exciting game. The girls won; but it was very close.

We stopped for a relaxed lunch which was followed by a short film before we began our rehearsals.

Following this hard work, they needed a reward; no, no sweets this time. We brought out the games, the big ones and the smaller ones. We also put out the small pool table, the small soccer table and the shuffleboard that we had purchased for the previous conference. We had a few rounds of the card game sets; not everyone wanted to play against Shira, but those who dared lost. She was still unbeatable.

Roni and Maya had attended a gymnastic class during the school year. They practiced their somersaults in the grandchildren's room on the carpet instead of joining the games.

We wanted the children to have a lot of energy when they put on the play for their parents, so this time we let them pig out with ice cream, m&m's and some sweets.

Afterwards they did a dress rehearsal. I was so pleased and proud of them that I almost cried.

As soon as all the parents were present, they took their seats in the living room to watch the performance. This time the participants were even better than during the rehearsals.

The performers received a lot of applause from the enthusiastic audience, followed by hugs and kisses. The parents were then invited to view the paintings on the wall and to see the new puzzle that the children had prepared.

When everyone calmed down, while some of the children

played some tunes on the piano, we set up the buffet table so that we could partake of a light supper together. Afterwards, the participants and their parents collected their things and left with their shopping bags filled with the treasures of the two days; the house was calm and quiet again.

THE PLAY

The Impressionists

<u>Characters:</u>

Shani - host of the exposition

Tamir - piano recitalist

Ido - piano recitalist

Dotan 1 - usher

Dotan 2 - guitar recitalist

Shira - art critic

Maya - young rich girl to see exposition

Roni - young rich girl to see exposition

Ori - art lover

Eran - art lover

First Scene

The show is about to begin. The usher is getting everyone seated.

Dotan 1: This way, please.

Shira: I was promised the best seat in the house.

Dotan 1: I will do my best.

Shira: Your best is not good enough.

Dotan 1: Please follow me.

Shira: I must make sure that I could see and hear everything.

Dotan 1: Yes, yes. I will find you a good seat.

Shira: I'll have you know that I am this country's best art critic.

Dotan 1: How about this seat in the front row?

Shira: All right. I guess it will do.

Dotan: *Playing two parts. One the usher and the other the guitar player. He is talking to himself.*

Dotan 1: Usher, Can I help you to your seat.

Dotan 2: No. I can find my own seat, thank you. *To the audience:* How could he, who is me show me to my seat.

Dotan 1: There's a seat for you with the rest of the performers near the piano.

Dotan 2: Thank you.

Dotan 1: May I show you two beautiful ladies to your seat.

Maya and Roni, *smiling. Yes, they say in chorus.* We hope you give us good seats. We booked well in advance.

He shows them two seats but each one wants to sit in the other one's seat. They keep going back and forth. Dotan becomes angry and puts one at one end and the other at the other end. When he goes away, they go back to their original seats and are quiet.

Maya and Roni together: This was fun. Now we can enjoy the show.

Dotan 1: I'll be right with you two. Running and trying to do many things at once. Yes, now I can show you to your seats. Can I have your tickets?

Eran: Ori, give him the tickets.

Ori: Me, I don't have the tickets.

Eran: Of course, you do

Ori: No, you took them.

Dotan 1: I will have to ask you to leave if you don't have the tickets.

Eran: Of course, we have the tickets. The only question is, where has Ori put them? Think back Ori. When was the last time you saw the tickets?

Ori: I can't remember.

Eran: You can't remember who has the tickets. You can't remember when you last saw them. What do you remember?

Ori: What I remember? I just remembered. I put the tickets in your pocket.

Eran: What? Are you stupid? Why would you put the tickets in my pocket?

Ori: Because I knew that if I put them in my pocket, I would forget, so I put them in your pocket.

Eran puts his hand into his pocket and of course, he finds the tickets.

Even before Ori and Eran are seated Ido and Tamir come pushing in.

Dotan 1: Please, wait and I will seat you in a minute.

Ido: We'll sit ourselves thank you.

Tamir: It's okay. We know where to sit.

Dotan 1: I'm the usher and I will seat you if you don't mind.

Ido: Please don't waste our precious time.

Dotan 1: And I say that you must wait until I seat you.

Tamir: You don't understand.

Dotan 1: No, you don't understand.

Ido: You must let us through, now.

Tamir: I will call Safta.

Dotan 1: And I will call Saba.

Ido: For the last time, please let us through.

Tamir: Please, we have not finished tuning up.

Dotan 1: Tuning up? For what?

Tamir: We are the pianists. We must go to the piano to prepare. We are part of the program.

Dotan1: Piano! Pianists? Why didn't you say so?

Ido: Why didn't you ask?

Scene II

Shani walks in and sits down facing the audience.

Shani: Welcome, welcome! I am so happy to see such a nice audience. Let me tell you about the program for today. First, I will speak about Monet and the Impressionists, then our two wonderful pianists will each play a short piece. Stand up, boys, and take a bow so that the audience can see you properly. Thank you, you may sit down. The pianists will be followed by the guitarist who will play a song. Dotan, take a bow.

Now before we have our short break, I will call out the names of each Impressionist and our cast will point the artist out, one by one on the wall.

Thank you for pointing out our Impressionists. We will have a short break while our pianists perform a small recital. Are you ready, boys?

First, Ido plays a piece and then Tamir.

Shani: I'm back. I hope you enjoyed the short recital. I was told to smile all the time and now my mouth is a little sore.

Now let me take you back in time. It is Paris, the years between 1860 and 1886. Monet and his friends, a small group of artists have become dissatisfied early in their careers with the academic teaching of historical or mythological subject matters.

When Monet arrives to Paris, he very quickly becomes bored painting indoors and together with some friends begins to paint outdoors. They are inspired by Boudin's idea of painting outdoors. During this period, all the artists would sketch their pieces and then finish the painting in the studios. Claude Monet had spent most of his childhood outdoors on the Normandy coast near Le Havre. He loved painting outdoors; to paint nature as he saw it with his own eyes.

The new paintings now reflected the colors of light upon water, trying to reproduce the effects of the sunlight. Monet and his group covered their canvases with many dabs of bright colors, to produce fragmented brilliance and contrasts of the sunlight and its beautiful reflections. Soon the forms began to lose their clear outlines and the traditional formal compositions were left behind.

In 1870 Napoleon III declares war on Prussia. Manet and Degas enlist as gunners. Monet moves to London to protect his family. Renoir becomes sick with dysentery. Bazille is killed and dies on the battlefield.

After the war, the painters return to Paris. The Impressionists continue with their new style but are still not accepted at the Salon. Degas becomes obsessed with ballet dancers. Renoir likes to paint women and Monet the outdoors.

Throughout their new style of painting, Monet and the rest of the group are influenced by the famous painter Édouard Manet. He encouraged them to adopt this approach but he himself accepted this style only in 1873.

Shira: Do you know how the Impressionists got their name?

Shani: I do but you are probably anxious to tell us so go ahead.

Shira: Can we ask the children first?

Shani: Okay.

Shira: Does anyone want to take a guess? No.

Monet and his friends, Paul Cezanne, Edgar Degas, Camille Pissarro, Pierre-Auguste Renoir, Alfred Sisley and Berthe Morisot, who, by the way, was a good friend and colleague of Edouard Manet but married his brother Eugene Manet, had all tried to have their work displayed at the official Salon of the French Academy but were rejected most of the time. In 1874, they decided to have their exhibition in a private place. A journalist, by the name of Louis Leroy, came to see the exhibition out of curiosity. Later, he wrote in a satirical magazine Le Charivari that Monet's painting was only an impression sunrise. The group liked this name and soon adopted it because their intention was to display the visual "impressions." They held seven subsequent shows, the last one was in 1886. During all that time, they continued to develop their own personal and individual styles.

Shani: Thank you, Shira. That was very informative. I just want to add that by the mid-1880s the Impressionist group had begun to dissolve as each painter increasingly pursued his own interest. However, the group had accomplished a revolution in the history of art, providing the groundwork for the Postimpressionist artists that followed.

Now let me just give you a point or two about each one.

Edouard Manet (1832-1883), His Luncheon on the grass in 1863, caused great controversy and influenced the Impressionists.

Claude Monet (1840-1926), The founder of French Impressionist painting. The leading figure in the group.

Auguste Renoir (1841-1910), An important painter in the development of the Impressionist style. He also liked to paint beautiful women.

Camille Pissarro (1831-1903), Pissarro is the only artist to have exhibited his work in all eight Paris Impressionist exhibitions, from 1874 to 1886. He was the father figure of the group.

Paul Cezanne (1839-1906), Cezanne struggled alone and was last to be recognized. The critics called his work ugly, but they were proved to be completely wrong. He was part of the Impressionists team that laid the foundation for a new generation of modern paintings.

Edgar Degas (1834-1917), Degas was one of the founders of the Impressionists who liked to paint dancers.

Berthe Morisot (1841-1895), A member of the Impressionist painters in Paris who in 1864 exhibited in the Salon de Paris.

Alfred Sisley (1839-1899), He was the most consistent of the Impressionists in his dedication to painting landscapes.

Frederic Bazille (1841-1870), Bazille was a close friend of Monet, Sisley and Manet. He was generous and helped his friends when they were in need. He was only 23 when he painted his famous works.

Now our pianists will play something together and we will finish this program with a piece played on the electric guitar by our young musician, Dotan.

Following Dotan's short piece Shani tells everyone that they are invited to see the exhibition.

Supplement

To add some children humor to the performance , I told Shani that she must smile all evening and she did; Dotan was funny with his two hats, playing the double roles of usher and guitar performer; Shira played her part well, from time to time adjusting her red beret; Eran and Ori were funny when they couldn't find their tickets; Tamir and Ido had a hard time getting past Dotan; and our two young, rich, spoiled females Maya and Roni made the participants laugh.

During the performance, I asked for two-time outs.

Remember the sixteen white t-shirts that we bought! We found a beautiful reproduction of Monet's famous painting Impression Sunrise. We printed out the picture from the internet and had this reproduction printed on all the t-shirts. During the time out we distributed the t-shirts. All the participants, their fathers, Shalom and two younger cousins put the t-shirts on; the impression was sensational.

During the second time out, we gave the mothers the Monet watches that we had bought at the Thyson Museum shop in Madrid. They were very happy when they received them, but I do not know how successful they really were because we never saw any of them using them. I guess you cannot always be a winner.

WORKSHOP II

HANUKKAH

8.12.2010

Previously

As you may recall, Workshop 1 followed a few months after Conference 1. I suppose that we were so happy that we had successfully accomplished the two-day difficult undertaking that we decided to try a one-day affair. Although the children were young, we wanted to start introducing a little learning with a little less playing and listening to small lectures.

Workshop 2 held three years after Workshop 1, was also held during Hanukkah. We had come a long way since then. The small chairs were now gone. The lectures had become an integral part of each meeting. We had similar topics this

Hanukkah as we used during the last workshop but a little more sophisticated.

Preparations

The dining room table was extended and covered with a festive Hanukkah tablecloth. At the center stood a nice bouquet of flowers that I had bought especially for this occasion. Besides the flowers stood our Menorah and close by, 9 Hanukkah candles waiting to be lit.

There were some other Hanukkah decorations, including a dreidel, a four-sided spinning top, played during Hanukkah. Each side bears a different letter in Hebrew standing for Nes Gadol Haya Po – meaning a Big Miracle Occurred Here (Israel). Some of these dreidels that are manufactured abroad change the fourth letter to mean there instead of here. There was also a plate with Hanukkah chocolate coins and a magazine with Hanukkah fun activities.

The two worktables also took on the festive look of Hanukkah, with new decorative place mats. The ones that we had used in the past conferences were given to the children to take home. Today, on these pretty place mats, we placed big, colorful disposable plates and festive napkins.

Wednesday 8.12.2010

The children arrived in a happy mood, noisy as always and excited as each one took his seat at the table. This time we had fresh bagels with cream cheese and a variety of freshly cut up vegetables together with the chocolate milk. Those who did not want the white cheese, used the creamy chocolate spread.

When we finished partaking of our light meal, the tables were cleared and we leaped into our first project: each participant constructed his own individual Menorah or as we call it here in Israel, Hanukkiah. This was no small task and we started early so that the artistic creations would be completed and dry for the candle lighting in the evening. The children worked happily, chatting, and helping one another. As soon as all the 9 Menorahs were completed, they were put on the trays to dry.

We then went into the living room where Shalom gave them a lecture about the Jewish population around the globe. On the small table, were flags of different countries in the world that we had downloaded from the computer. Shalom pointed out on the world map the country and the different flag. The children found this activity very interesting as some of them were familiar with many of the flags.

When I had first thought of the next project of having the children design their own t-shirts, I thought it would be a great idea and something unique. I bought white plain t-shirts for the girls and black t-shirts for the boys. I also bought several accessories; special sewing needles with big holes and dull points; nice buttons for decorations, interesting logos that included: soccer team crests, butterflies and flowers. I also bought a variety of colored threads. The project turned out to be much less successful and disappointing. Most of them were still too young; the majority did not have the slightest idea how to hold a needle in their hand nor how to thread it. I ended up doing most of the work for them. Some just took the plain t-shirts and some of the logos home. Dotan was very original: since he did not know how to sew, he designed his t-shirt with the scissors. He cut off the sleeves and cut out some of the front and made a nice, light shirt which came out artistic and that he made good use for a long time.

After lunch, the children played with the big games, the small games, the card games and the wooden blocks from the conferences. Since it was Hanukkah, they also played with the dreidels.

Then we had a Hanukkah quiz which Shalom had prepared that proved educational and entertaining. They knew most of the answers so that they all participated.

To refuel our energies, we had a quick fruit break and then there was the screening of a full-length film of Laurel and Hardy that made everyone roar with laugher.

While the children went back to the games Shalom was busy in the dining room. They were not allowed to see what he was doing until he was ready. And then the most exciting moment of the day had arrived!

Behold the sight that greeted our eyes! Shalom had arranged all the Menorahs that the children had prepared, to form one big Menorah. He put one candle in each Menorah so that we had in all nine candles, eight for the eighth candle lighting of Hanukkah and one for the Shamash. The children were so proud of their accomplishments.

We lit all the eight candles of Hanukkah together, chanting the prayer. Then we sang all the beautiful Hanukkah songs that we all knew by heart and partook of the Hanukkah goodies.

CONFERENCE V

SMILE WITH SCIENCE

July 29-30, 2011

A few months before conference 5

LIKE THE MONET napkins triggered off the idea for Conference Number 4, the Impressionist, the idea for Conference 5 began with extraordinary t-shirts.

Shalom and I were in San Francisco where he was attending an International Scientific Meeting. Our hotel was located close to the beautiful harbor and its many delightful shops. As you have learned by now, whenever we were abroad, I was always on the lookout for special souvenirs for the grandchildren. I was walking along the harbor when in one of the window shops they were advertising white t-shirts with the logo of the famous

San Francisco bridge. I walked in and headed for the t-shirts. When I saw the price, I asked the salesman why they were so expensive. Well, he said, take one outside see what happens.

I stepped outside and behold something extra-ordinary occurred. I knew right then that I wanted them. I went back inside and asked the salesman if I would get a discount for 11 t-shirts. No, he replied. The price was already on special sale at 30 dollars a t-shirt. My mind was busy doing fast math converting the total cost into shekel and came up with a four-digit sum. This time it was too much.

But I just could not get the t-shirts out of my head. I went back day after day to look at them. I really wanted them! I knew that I could not go back to Israel without them. I asked Shalom to come to see them. He thought that they were very impressive but way too expensive.

That same night, I woke up and was struck with a brilliant idea. I could not wait for the morning to tell Shalom. During breakfast I told him that we should buy the t-shirts because they would be an important item for our next grandchildren conference on the topic that was the closest to his heart, science. I had used the magic word and already in his mind he was thinking how much he could teach them on this subject.

On the way home from San Francisco we stopped over in Montreal to visit my mother and sister and the rest of the family. We had a nice visit as always and bought a few more things for the conference.

Day One

Everything is in place. It is almost 10 a.m. Shalom and I are ready to receive our nine young participants to Grandchildren Conference Number 5. I am feeling apprehensive and nervous. This happens to me every year before the children arrive. The same worries race through my mind. Will everything be okay? Will the children cooperate? Will this year live up to par?

Shalom and I are having a cup of coffee, trying to relax before the participants arrive.

"I can't believe that this will be our fifth conference already."

"It really is amazing! When you first came up with this wild idea, I was sure that it would be a one-time affair."

"I remember our first conference was so simple. It was a plain sleepover with games and videos. The children were so small.

We were so exhausted at the end of the two days that we were sure that it would be the first and last sleepover."

"Not sleepover, Conference."

"Yes, Conference. Then, the second conference had a program and by the time we organized Conference Number 3, we reached even higher standards. I am so nervous today. I didn't spend enough time preparing this year".

"Every time, it's the same thing. Stop worrying, we have a wonderful program."

"But is it as good as last year's?

"It's even better."

"But won't the children be disappointed? Last year we held the conference just before our renovations. We called that conference the Impressionists. We put up many paintings of the Impressionist on the wall. Remember all the decorations and color. Our living room and dining room were transformed into an art gallery."

"This year we have such a great theme that they won't miss the decorations."

"I hope you're right. "

"I know I am."

"I hear the doorbell."

As usual everyone was in good humor. After the individual photos on the lazy boy in the living room were taken, we all gathered around the two tables to partake of our bagels and chocolate milk.

This time I opened the conference by welcoming the children.

Yaffa

I am happy that we were able to convene this conference which I hope will be even more successful than the last one. As usual Saba and I worked very hard. The schedule is full, but we hope that you will find everything interesting. This is the result of having a grandfather a scientist and a grandmother who has problems sleeping. As you have learned by now, the purpose of our conferences is not only to get together and have fun but also to use the time to learn new and difficult things together in a fun way.

To succeed this year, we need your best behavior and a lot of cooperation. It is possible that a few of you are already familiar with some of the difficult subjects, even so it is still advisable to listen to the way Saba explains them in his easy to understand manner.

You are probably curious to know what we have in the program today. Of course, there are many surprises that I will not reveal now. It is always more exciting to look forward to surprises.

So, what do we have in the program that I can reveal. We will have our 36-piece puzzle, prepare a memory game and yes, of course, have a bazaar. We will have special desserts, a good Shabbat dinner, many goodies and tomorrow we will have supper with your parents.

You see, we have a lot of things lined up for you, but I will leave you curious. You know the important, famous scientists were all curious. Curiosity is a necessary characteristic if you want to be a good scientist. When a person docs not know what is to follow, especially when expecting good things, the mood is favorable and so is the behavior.

Enough with the talk, let us begin by going into the living room to find a place in front of the television. There are comfortable seats for everyone so no need to push. One more thing, I forgot to mention that today, each time when we watch a short film we will have popcorn or a popsicle. From this minute on we are going to smile with science. Let us see how many smart and interesting things you can learn and remember. And do not forget, a big surprise is awaiting you.

The children quietly found places to sit and watch a few small science short films that I had taped. I was pleasantly surprised that they did not complain about the films. Sometimes I underestimate them.

Following the short science films, Shalom asked some questions and was pleased that they had paid attention to the documentaries and were now able to answer many of his questions correctly.

Then, we went to the first surprise that awaited them. The girls went into the grandchildren's room while the boys stayed in the living room. They all changed into the same white t-shirts, except that each one had the imprint of a different scientist. Each participant now looked at himself in the mirror and then walked around introducing himself as the character in the picture.

So, who was who?
Shani: *Benjamin Franklin*
Dotan: *Theodor Maiman*
Tamir: *Charles Robert Darwin*
Ido: *Louis Pasteur*
Ori: *Albert Einstein*
Eran: *Galileo Galilei*
Shira: *Isaac Newton*
Maya: *Wilhelm Roentgen*
Roni: *Leonardo da Vinci*
We could tell by the looks on their faces that they already

felt smarter. Attired in their new t-shirts, they went into the living room and found their seats in an orderly manner.

Shalom

I want to tell each one of you about the important scientist who you will be representing later at the discussion around the table; a humoristic dialogue that Safta has written for you. These men have accomplished many important things, but I will mention briefly what they did.

Leonardo da Vinci lived from 1452 to 1519. He was an Italian genius and one of the greatest painters of all time. He was also a brilliant engineer who left many scientific inventions. His drawings of the human body were very important in understanding its classification.

Galileo Galilei lived from 1564 to 1642. He was an Italian scientist who is considered the father of the scientific methods. He was the father of modern physics and the first person to use a telescope for observational astronomy.

Isaac Newton lived from 1642 to 1727. He was an English mathematician and physicist. Today he is considered one of the two greatest and most influential scientists of all time. He discovered the law of gravitation and the laws of motion and is known for other important contributions in science.

Benjamin Franklin lived from 1706 to 1790. He was an American politician and scientist. He was one of the Founding Fathers of the United States. He was an inventor, a political philosopher, a diplomat and a scientist who contributed significantly to the discovery of electricity. (His picture is on the US $100 bill).

Charles Darwin lived from 1809 to 1882. He was an Englishman who is known as one of the most influential biologists in human history. His evolution theory suggesting that all species of life have descended over time from common ancestors is scientifically accepted today.

Louis Pasteur lived from 1822 to 1895. He was a French biologist and chemist. He is considered as one of the fathers of microbiology. He discovered the principles of vaccination and pasteurization. His research proved that germs cause disease. His discoveries have saved many lives.

Wilhelm Roentgen lived from 1845 to 1923. He was a German mechanical engineer and physicist. He detected the electromagnetic radiation known today as X-rays. For this achievement, he received the first Nobel Prize in physics in 1901.

Albert Einstein lived from 1879 to 1955. He was a German-born citizen of the world. He was a theoretical physicist who is considered one of the two great physicists of all time. His famous formula ($E=mc^2$) is known almost by all. His special and general theories of relativity were a big step in advancing physics. He was a pioneer in a few important scientific subjects. He received the Nobel Prize in 1921.

Theodore Maiman lived from 1927 to 2007. He was an American engineer and physicist who built the first laser in 1960. He received a patent for the laser.

From their intelligent questions, we knew that they had, again, been listening.

Then another surprise awaited them: sleeveless t-shirts that we had bought; black for the boys, two turquoise for the older girls and two light green for the two younger ones. They were perfect for the hot day.

After they had changed into the new sleeveless t-shirts, they found their place at the table and each one took four pieces of the puzzle to paint. This time I had printed out many objects dealing with science. The children were so happy painting the pieces, talking, laughing, and at times lending a hand to his or her fellow participant. When all the pieces were complete, they put them on the tray to dry.

It was time to stretch our legs and do some exercise. I put on some music, we got into pairs and we danced the rock and roll dance. This time it was a success and we all had a good time.

Following the fun with the exhausting dance, everyone was ready for lunch. This was followed by another science documentary, this time with delicious homemade popsicles.

Then, to relax, Shalom and I told them some children jokes that I had found on the internet. This put all of us in a good and happy mood; perfect for the preparation of the memory game of our nine scientists. On two blocks the children wrote out the name of the scientist and on the other two blocks they made some likeness of two of their inventions. In all there were 36 blocks.

The memory game

Leonardo da Vinci: inside the human body; a harp.
Galileo Galilei: telescope; pendulum.
Isaac Newton: apple; prism.
Benjamin Franklin: kite; bifocal glasses.
Charles Darwin: big turtle; small turtle.
Louis Pasteur: vaccine; chicken.
Wilhelm Roentgen: picture of hand bones; x-ray.
Albert Einstein: $E = mc^2$; gravitation.
Theodore Maiman: laser; engineer and physicist.

This task went well and was concluded quickly. While the wooden blocks were put to dry, the children painted some artistic design on the white shopping bags that I had prepared for them. By the time this project was completed, the wooden blocks were dry enough to play the memory game. The blocks were placed upside down and each one had to choose a pair: the name of the scientist and the block connected to him. We played a few rounds and by the time that we ended several games, they knew the names of the nine scientists well.

We then went back to the living room and watched another short science documentary, this time with popcorn.

Soon it was wash up time, pajama pictures and just some precious minutes to play some quick games before our Shabbat Dinner.

All the girls put on scarfs and helped me light the Shabbat candles. We took our time partaking of the good food. We were all tired. It had been a long day.

Each participant brushed his teeth, prepared his sleeping quarters and as a reward we put on some funny films instead of a science documentary.

DAY TWO

Once they all had breakfast, brushed their teeth and put the bedding out of the way, another surprise awaited them. New t-shirts; the boys green, the girls yellow. We had a very busy day ahead and we got started right away.

The first thing on the schedule was the carrying out of a few experiments that I had loaded down from the internet. For the first experiment, I had especially bought white flowers. Did you know that if you put white flowers in a vase of water with food coloring overnight the petals change color? If you leave the color in longer more color will fill the petals. I did not know this either and I am not sure that this really works. I had put the flowers in a vase Thursday evening and had especially bought food coloring but throughout Friday and Saturday, the flowers remained white. Maybe I did something wrong.

The second experiment was carried out by Maya and Roni. They took a bowl of water and put a few matchsticks. Then they added some liquid soap and the matchsticks were supposed to shoot across the surface, but they did not. At this time, I became a bit worried.

Then Dotan and Shira took a glass of water, put one straw inside the glass and the other one touching the outside of the glass; Dotan sucked on both straws and no water came up. Then we used two new straws and Shira did the same experiment and she too was successful. A sigh of relief; success at last.

Up next were Eran and Ori. They took a glass and filled it with soda water. They threw in 5 raisins and after one minute the raisins began moving up and down in the glass. Success again!

Tamir took two balls, a large one and a smaller one. He put the small ball on top of the large one and dropped them together at the same time. The energy from the bottom ball (the big one) was transferred to the second ball, causing the small ball on top to bounce up high. He was so successful that everyone tried this trick and it worked for everyone. Another success.

Next, up was Ido. He took a pitcher and filled it with water. Then he took a glass and put a crumpled-up napkin inside the glass. He put the glass upside down into the water in the pitcher. Then he took the glass out and placed it right side up. The napkin was supposed to be completely dry, but it was almost dry. Not a total failure.

Shani took an empty water bottle and filled it with hot water, swirled it around to make the bottle hot and then she poured the water out. She refilled a quarter of the bottle with hot water and placed a blown-up balloon over the top. Then she filled a bowl with ice water and placed the bottle in the bowl. The air was drawn out from the balloon and the balloon was pulled into the bottle.

Another success.

Shalom had planned to bring a prism from work and show the children what happens when it is placed in the sun. The prism had not been available, so instead, he took a glass of water and some white paper and placed it near the window. He held the glass of water above the paper and we all watched as the sunlight passed through the glass, refracted and formed a rainbow of colors on the sheet of paper.

Following these small experiments, it was time for the biggest surprise of all, the expensive San Francisco t-shirts. As soon as they all changed into the new, expensive t-shirts, we went upstairs to the second floor. As they stepped out to the balcony one, by one, out into the sun, the San Francisco Bridge logo on the t-shirt changed slowly from black and white to color. Everyone was thrilled. They had never seen such t-shirts. They promised to wear them with care and show them off to all their friends.

When we came downstairs again, everyone changed back into the green and yellow t-shirts. They folded up the San Francisco t-shirts carefully and put them in their bags. I was happy to see how nicely they handled these expensive t-shirts.

Then we all went into the living room and Shalom and I discussed the different inventions throughout the years. They all listened very carefully; they did not know that some of the inventions and inventors were also new to us, and of course, we did not tell them.

In between our activities, I made sure that there would be lots of cut up fruit and vegetable that disappeared quickly.

It was time for relaxation: the children had worked hard, and they deserved something easy. Each one received a small canvas and made a painting of his choice using paint brushes and water paints.

Then we had a science quiz with questions about space, physics, technology and animals that Shalom had prepared for them. For this we took out our white board. The children were divided into two groups. As always when we had a competition the participation and excitement were notable.

After a satisfying and relaxing lunch, the children put on their white t-shirts with the logos of the scientists. We handed out the typed pages with the one scene play "A Small Debate" that I had written. The full play is presented at the end of this section.

The first reading was slow, and I had to bring out the sweets to boost up their energies. Then we went through the reading again and it was much better. We did it one last time and filmed it.

The children needed a reward for their hard work. We brought out all the big and small games and while they were busy, Shalom and I prepared the bazaar. This was always the part in the program that the children looked forward to. The bazaar was loud and very exciting. We had a sell out and the children were very pleased.

Following the bazaar, we all went into the living room and watched the documentary on Lucy, several hundred pieces of a fossilized bone representing 40 percent of the skeleton of a female of the hominin species. "Lucy was discovered in 1974 in Africa. It is dated back to about 3.2 million years. The skeleton represents a small skull akin to that of non-hominin apes plus evidence of a walking gait that was bipedal and upright, akin to that of humans. Lucy acquired her name from the song "Lucy in the Sky with Diamonds" by the Beatles, which was played loudly and repeatedly in the expedition camp all evening after the excavation team's first day of work on the recovery site. Thus, Lucy became famous worldwide". This information was taken from Wikipedia.

To our surprise, the children loved it. I guess they were tired and needed to relax or maybe the good tasting popsicles helped.

The parents arrived at 7 p.m. We set up the tables and had a nice supper together.

It had been a very successful conference after all, as Shalom had reassured me when I had had my doubts. This conference was as good as the previous one. The children had learned interesting and difficult things. It had been an educational, high level conference and we were so proud of our participants and ourselves. They had walked away smiling.

THE PLAY

A few words about "A Small Debate."

Seated around the table are nine distinguished scientists, discussing their important work that they had left to mankind. Each one tries to impress the others with his important work and legacy. Some parts are humoristic as each one tries to point out, in a non-arrogant, way his good work.

<u>The participants</u>

Leonardo da Vinci (1452-1519) - Roni
Galileo Galilei (1564-1642) -Eran
Isaac Newton (1642-1727) -Shira
Benjamin Franklin (1706-1790) -Shani
Charles Darwin (1809-1882) -Tamir
Louis Pasteur (1822-1895) -Ido
Wilhelm Roentgen (1845-1923) -Maya
Albert Einstein (1879-1955) -Ori
Theodore Maiman (1927-2007) -Dotan

Newton: *Turning to Galileo*: Do you know who I am?

Galileo: Of course, I know. Your name appears on your t-shirt…, and don't think that you are the most important person here. You were lucky that you were born the same year that I died. I prepared the foundation for you and you were able to continue my line of thought.

Newton: I do not deny this. Tell me, who is sitting next to you claiming that he is more important than the rest of us?

Einstein: I'll have you know that I am even more important than Newton.

Franklin: Yes…yes. All of us are important and all of us made significant contributions to science. The proof that I am right, is the fact that all of us were invited to this Grandchildren Conference "Smile With Science".

da Vinci: Grandchildren Conference? What is it? I existed before all of you and in my time, there were no such things. In my time children went to do hard labor.

Maiman: It's been only a few years since I passed away. I attended many conferences on physics. I heard about conferences in chemistry, art, architecture, medicine, almost every theme, but I never heard about Grandchildren Conferences.

(everybody speaks together loudly)

Darwin: Quiet! Why are you so noisy? You forgot that you are at a Grandchildren Conference! Everyone is supposed to behave properly.

Roentgen: You all know how important I am, yet I sit quietly waiting for my turn to speak.

Pasteur: So, we already heard how much all of us are important. I suggest that each one tell us what he has contributed to mankind and why this is so significant.

Franklin: I am the oldest grandchild and therefore I shall chair this meeting.

Maiman: I am not much younger than you are. Therefore, I suggest to cochair this meeting and if someone forgets some important information about himself, I can help him remember. My mother always said that I have a good memory and today I can put it to good use.

Franklin: Okay, but on condition that you will help only when I ask you to. Agreed?

Maiman: Agreed.

Franklin: Good, we will all speak according to the chronological order. Da Vinci, you lived before all of us therefore you begin.

da Vinci: I am referred to as the genius of the Renaissance. I knew almost everything, and I was interested in almost everything. I painted, I sculptured, I played music, I was a great engineer, as well as a scientist trying to experiment in things that were dealt with much later. Most of my great ideas were not understood during my lifetime. Today, everyone knows my name. I have become famous around the world.

Roentgen: Everybody knows that you painted the Mona Lisa. This is the most famous painting in the world.

Maiman: Don't forget the famous Last Supper that hangs in the convent in Milano.

da Vinci: It's good that you mentioned it because after I painted the last supper the prince declared a harp competition. For this occasion, 80 people, including myself, attended. I of course, came with the harp that I had constructed myself and I played so well that I won the competition.

Maiman: Today you are known by most people for your paintings, although you were also a scientist, an engineer, an inventor, a sculptor, an architect and now I learn that you were also a musician. Did I miss something?

Franklin: Maiman you talk too much. Let us continue with Galileo.

Galileo: I am the father of modern science. It was I who said that the language of science is mathematics and the scientific theories should be judged by experiments. It is through experiment that the scientist could test if a theory is correct or wrong. I have many stories. I lived during a difficult time for a scientist. Today it is hard to understand these difficulties because science has the freedom to proclaim and publicize new ideas and concepts. In my time I had many difficulties with the powerful influence of the church; I was almost executed for my strong scientific beliefs, but I always knew that I was right.

Pasteur: Stop rattling, we do not have time. Just tell us what you did?

Maiman: I read about you that you gave in to the church and said that the Earth is not moving and that the Sun and our planets are circling the Earth because this is what the church wanted you to say.

Galileo *(angrily)*: And what would you have done in my place? Should I have been burned at the stake like Giordano Bruno and others?

(everyone begins to talk noisily at the same time)

Darwin: Quiet! You forgot that we are at a Grandchildren Conference!

Galileo: Sorry, I would like to continue later.

Franklin: All right. I believe that now it is your turn Newton.

Newton: I am considered by the scientists as a great mathematician and one of the best physicists of all time. I invented the mathematics that explain the physical laws of motion. Like Galileo has mentioned, the language of physics is mathematics and I am the one who invented this novel language for physics. I also discovered many important matters in optics which I carried out with a prism, such as the fact that the light has many colors.

I am sure that everyone has heard about the "apple story". I was investigating the force of gravitation and it is said that while I was sitting under a tree an apple fell on my head. This story could have been true because the force of gravitation acting on the apple causes the apple to fall. I assure you that many apples have fallen from the tree, but I have never had an apple fall on my head.

Franklin: Very interesting. Now I believe that it is my turn. I also have a long list of accomplishments. I was one of the founding fathers of the United States of America; I was a politician, a diplomat, a scientist, an inventor and a musician. I created the first library and the first fire department in the USA.

As a scientist I did research on electricity before we knew what electricity was. I discovered that during a thunderstorm there are electrical charges at large.

I invented the bifocal glasses so that people could see better from short and far distances. This invention is also used today.

I introduced the idea of payment by the hour because time is money. This is also in use today. By the way, you can see my face on the 100 USA dollar bills.

What else can I tell you? I was the USA ambassador to

France. I returned to the USA with the idea of freedom and I introduced this into our constitution.

I dedicated my free time to science.

Maiman: You talk so much that one may think that you are the most important person here.

Darwin: Enough with this nonsense! We already agreed that all of us are important, otherwise we would not be here today. Now it is my turn and I also have many things to say.

The development of the human being is not trivial at all. Until I wrote my work on the evolution, no one understood the development of life on Earth. What is evolution? Evolution is how the different species developed during millions of years from one primitive creature. The theory of evolution changed the principles of biology and influenced the sciences in general. I am referred to as the father of modern biology.

What brought me to my research on evolution? I studied to be a medical doctor, but I did not like it so much. One day I received an offer to join a long voyage, on a ship named The Beagle, where I was supposed to do some research. We landed on distant and isolated places and for the first time in my life I saw strange animals and birds. I became very excited when I saw the big turtles and other strange creatures. When I returned from my long journey, I wrote many books describing what I had seen. I soon became very famous. I came to the right conclusion, that is also accepted today, namely, that the different species on our planet were developed according to their environment and only the fittest survived.

Pasteur: You spoke enough. Now it is my turn.

Franklin *(loudly)*: I thought that I am the chairman for our discussions.

(the participants again begin to speak together and loudly)

Darwin: Quiet! You have forgotten again where you are.

Pasteur: Sorry, the chairman is right. Can I begin?

Franklin: Okay, go ahead.

Pasteur: I invented the first vaccine. I am the father of microbiology. I have discovered and carried out famous research with microbes. I first began my research in chemistry investigating the properties of materials, but during my work I found "the microbes" and I became an enthusiastic "microbe hunter."

Now I would like to unfold how I found the secret of the vaccine. I was asked to investigate some chicken disease called cholera chicken. I worked hard and became very dedicated to this problem. I discovered that germs are causing this disease and I asked my assistant to accumulate these microbes. This is a horrible disease. We accumulated a lot of these tissue cultures in our laboratory and I asked my assistant to clean the places every week. I also asked him to inject a few drops of the one-week culture into a few sick chickens. These chickens already looked bad and I expected them to die shortly, but to my surprise the chickens were well and happy. I injected a few drops of this culture with microbes into the two chickens that had completely recovered from the disease and they also were eating and crowing happily. And this is how the vaccine was discovered; a little quantity of microbes made the body resistant to this disease.

Maiman: I read that you also invented something to make the milk safe for drinking and it is named after you.

Pasteur: This is correct, but I did not finish my presentation yet. I found in the milk some dangerous microbes and suggested a way to get rid of them. The process is called pasteurization, named after me.

Franklin: Every story that we hear today is exciting. I am very proud of all of us. We were very clever. Roentgen now it is your turn.

Roentgen: I discovered the x-ray, sometimes referred to the roentgen rays. One day when I opened the drawer of my desk, I found that some film plates, that I was using in my experiments, were blurred. I was surprised how the rays that I had created in my experiment reached the drawer. Then I understood that they penetrated my desk. I was curious to see if these rays could penetrate my hand as well and to my surprise, I saw the bones of my hand on the film. I also looked how the rays penetrated my wife's hand and saw her bones as well.

These X-rays are used in medicine today. Thanks to my invention, we can investigate the human body without cutting it open. For my research I received the first Noble prize in physics in 1901.

Galileo: Nobel? Remind me who is Nobel?

Maiman: Nobel was a scientist who invented the dynamite. He became very rich and when he died, he left his money to the Swedish government to create the most prestigious prize, the Nobel Prize, that began in 1901 and it is still awarded today.

Can I add something about Roentgen?

Roentgen: Yes, please do.

Maiman: The medical applications of the X-rays are well known, but there are also important industrial applications. These rays can test different components of an instrument and detect small cracks or tiny holes that can cause the instrument not to function properly or even to break.

Franklin: Thank you Maiman. Now we expect Einstein to speak.

Einstein: The thing that I always enjoyed the most was to think. As a child, I always thought what causes things to act. My father dealt with repairing electrical instruments. When I was in his shop, I learned about electricity. As a child when I was sick, my father bought me a compass that always showed the north direction. I am wondering if anyone can explain my theory of relativity? You Maiman?

Newton: May I? I read your work Einstein and I was excited that you followed and generalized my theory.

Einstein: Do you agree Franklin?

Franklin: I wanted to explain but I will let Newton speak.

Newton: Thank you. Einstein invented the theory of relativity. He calculated and found that at very high velocities, almost the speed of light, the length shortens, and the time increases. Most important he showed that the mass, namely the weight of a body on earth, can transfer to energy following his simple and well-known equation $E=mc^2$. Einstein continued my theory of gravitation and explained many phenomena in our cosmos.

Einstein: Thank you very much Newton. You explained my theory clearly and exactly as I wanted to.

Franklin: Believe it or not, it is now your turn to speak Maiman.

Maiman: I built the first laser in the world in the year 1960. Einstein initiated the laser theory and after that, two physicists from Russia and one from the USA got the Nobel Prize for the laser theory. But I was the one who built the first laser, and this was not trivial at all. I was lucky to be a physicist and an engineer and therefore I could do it. My first laser was as big as my palm. Today there are huge lasers. Saba and Safta visited the biggest laser system in the world in Livermore, USA, which is as large as two football stadiums put together. The light from this laser is enormous.

When I built the laser, no one knew for what it would be useful. People said that the scientists have found a solution, but no one knew for what. Today, lasers are used in many fields besides physics; in medicine, in industry, to measure distances, in the supermarkets and so on.

Franklin: Now we have come to the end of our discussion. Does anyone have anything to add?

Galileo: I did not finish my talk. I did not tell you yet about the telescope and my observation of the stars in the sky at night. I was the first to discover more moons around our planets, just like the moon around the Earth. I started the laws of mechanics and I discovered the first law of Newton before he was born. I discovered the principle of relativity, before Einstein was born. I measured man's pulse rate with a pendulum before people were able to measure seconds. Pasteur you see that I also contributed something to medicine.

Darwin: I think that everybody spoke enough. Yesterday and today, we learned about science and how much we contributed to mankind.

WORKSHOP III

TEAMWORK

March 24, 2012

Long Distance Communication

THIS WORKSHOP WAS PREPARED with the participant's full cooperation and teamwork. With their long-distance collaboration, it turned out to be one of the most enjoyable and educational workshops. By the time we convened Workshop III, they were all ready and knew the material well. How did we do it?

Shalom and I were in Madrid during the month of February 2012. The weather was miserable with rain almost every day. Each morning Shalom went to work while I was in our room at the Residencia (the special guest house for Visiting Professors and students, close to one of the Polytechnique Universities in

Madrid where Shalom worked as a Visiting Professor). I had a lot of free time to think. One day I suddenly got a great idea; I was anxious for Shalom to come for lunch (that we had almost every day in the spacious and elegant dining room at the Residencia). As soon as he came into the room, I told him excitedly that I had a great idea for our next workshop. "Why not do a review of some of the important and famous historical personalities that the children had met during the five conferences and the two workshops?" Immediately Shalom became excited; to him anything dealing with education tops highest ranking. Once I got the go ahead signal from him, we began full speed ahead.

The first thing was to ask the children for their e-mail addresses so that I could correspond with them quickly. Remember that we are talking about the year 2012 when some of them were still very young and not everyone had a personal e-mail account. I had to approach the parents and ask them to open an account for those who did not have one. Once this procedure was settled, Shalom and I compiled a list of past personalities that we had met during our conferences and workshops; in all we made a list of 23 names:

Following, is our letter to the 9 participants that I sent on Friday the 17th of February 2012:

To all the participants of our conferences and workshops

We want to organize another workshop shortly after our return to Israel, but this time we need your help. We want to prepare a small review of some of the famous and important people about whom we learned during the past five conferences and two workshops in an interesting way. It is important to have your cooperation; all of you must participate. If one of you will not send in his reply quickly, this will hold every one up. Remember that we are "all for one and one for all" like the famous author, Alexandre Dumas wrote in his book "The Three Musketeers" which some of you are familiar with from the movie. We do not have too much time, so we must get going quickly. First, I need your e-mail addresses.

Within two days we received all the addresses; their cooperation, as well as that of their parents, was off to a good start.

Next, I sent each one the following list of names and e-mailed the first assignment to each one separately. Once we had everyone's reply, I e-mailed the second assignment and so it went. In total, there were 6 assignments and by the time we returned to Israel, the children had managed to complete them all. Following is the list of names.

Important names from our previous conferences:

- Albert Einstein
- Galileo Galilei
- Isaac Newton
- Leonardo da Vinci
- Theodore Maiman
- Charles Darwin
- Louis Pasteur
- Wilhelm Roentgen
- Benjamin Franklin
- Berthe Morisot
- Jean Frederic Bazille
- Claude Monet
- Edouard Manet
- Pierre Auguste Renoir
- Edgar Degas
- Paul Cezanne
- Camille Pissarro
- Alfred Sisley
- Francisco Goya
- Napoleon Bonaparte
- Vincent van Gogh
- Ludwig van Beethoven
- Fernando Botero

First Assignment

Each one must choose **3 names** that are familiar to him or to her from the list and send the names to me.

Second Assignment

From the three names that you picked, choose **one name** and send it to one of the other participants with **a copy to me.**

Third Assignment

Send **another name** to a different participant with a **copy to me.** You are now left with <u>one name</u> that you have not sent to anyone. Keep it for yourself and do not tell any of the other participants. In the meantime, only you, Saba and I know the name and we will save this until later.

Fourth Assignment

This time you must send your replies **only to me.**

Below is a list of 42 words or short phrases. **Choose 5 words or phrases** from the 42 and write to which conference or workshop the word or phrase belongs. For example, number 3 Lucy (documentary film about evolution – man ape) Conference 5:

1. The woman in green
2. Impression in the water

3. Lucy
4. San Francisco
5. The white board
6. Origami
7. Stamps
8. Chess
9. Sets - the card game
10. Memory game competition
11. The city of Paris
12. Louvre (museum)
13. Art critic
14. Soccer ball game
15. The Cookie story
16. Beads for necklaces
17. The Eiffel Tower
18. Eroica
19. What's with Botero?
20. The wager
21. The big turtle
22. The experiment succeeded
23. T-shirts from Portugal
24. The Hasmonean
25. The lighting of 9 Menorahs
26. Who cut the t-shirt?
27. So what if nobody knows how to sew?
28. Why is Shani smiling all the time
29. Where did Roni go?
30. Why does Dotan have 2 hats
31. To play the piano with four hands

32. Where are the tickets?

33. You have them!

34. Quiet, here people don't make noise

35. The Sower

36. The first paintings were done more than 30,000 years ago.

37. The modern picture the way it is known today was painted approximately 800 years ago.

38. The first stamp was issued approximately 170 years ago in England.

39. The game of chess was first introduced about 2000 years ago somewhere in the far east.

40. Chocolate monopoly.

41. Competition boys against girls – Goya.

42. Why is Eran wearing a hat?

Fifth Assignment

This time you must send your replies **just to me.**

Following is a list of the names of the Impressionists from Conference 4 and another list containing verses of two lines. Choose which 2-line verse belongs to which Impressionist and send the answer **to me.**

<u>The 9 Impressionists</u>

- Berthe Morisot
- Frederic Bazille
- Claude Monet

- Edouard Manet
- Pierre Auguste Renoir
- Edgar Degas
- Paul Cezanne
- Camille Pissarro
- Alfred Sisley

The two-line verses:

1. Painting women was his delight
Using the brush strokes just right.

2. A genius who did not receive his due
And only after death his fame grew.

3. An artist who began a new style (impression) that has grown.
Even today it is loved and well known.

4. A name that was almost the same
As the artist who then had much less fame.

5. Dancers were his favorite subjects
But he also painted many other objects.

6. Always helping a friend in need
He was a good friend indeed.

7. One woman among the nine
Whose paintings were so fine.

8. One Jew among the group
Who too was a good painter of this small troop.

9. One of the richest of the new trend
Died penniless at the end.

Sixth Assignment

Answers to **me only**

For each scientist from Conference 5, choose 1 word or phrase that is associated with him.

- Albert Einstein
- Galileo Galilei
- Sir Isaac Newton
- Leonardo da Vinci
- Theodor Maiman
- Charles Darwin
- Louis Pasteur
- Wilhelm Roentgen
- Benjamin Franklin

<u>List of Words</u>

Telescope, apple, kite, laser, X-ray, Beagle, relativity, radiation, pendulum, human body, differential calculus, bacteria, First Nobel Prize in Physics, photons, monkey, and yet it moves, vaccination, a scheme for flying, prism, ruby laser, electricity, an illustration of the bones of the hand, eye glasses, chickens, evolution, music lover (especially violin).

The children were very cooperative, more than we had expected. They tried to answer me as quickly as possible so that we could have all the replies before our return to Israel.

Preparations

The preparations took less time than usual. We had arranged most of the program in Madrid, bought many souvenirs, and even found a huge new surprise to bring home. During my correspondence with the participants I wrote them that they should expect something extremely big which I promised would provide a lot of fun. This of course made them even more anxious for the workshop.

We still had a few things left to buy when we returned: new towels, art supplies, and so on. I also still had the cooking, but we managed everything more quickly this time.

Saturday

The big day arrived! This time we were as anxious as the children to get started. Promptly at 10 a.m. they came.

After partaking of our usual morning snack, we immediately began our meeting. The children received their individual hand towels, small notebooks, a pencil case with pencils and erasers. They hung up their towels; the girls in one bathroom; the boys in the other. They drank some water and we were ready to begin this workshop.

We began with Assignments 4, 5 and 6.

Shalom

Assignment 4 - Shalom used the famous white board to make 7 columns, one for each of the five conferences and two workshops. The children were supposed to pick the number beside the word, or group of words appropriate for the conference or workshop from the list of words that we had sent them from Madrid. We went from the youngest to the oldest.

For the convenience of some of us, following is the list again:

1. The woman in green
2. Impression in the water
3. Lucy
4. San Francisco
5. the white board
6. origami
7. stamps
8. Chess
9. Sets - the card game
10. Memory game competition
11. The city of Paris
12. Louvre museum
13. Art critic
14. Soccer ball game
15. The Cookie story
16. Beads for necklaces
17. The Eiffel Tower
18. Eroica

Conference I	Conference II	Conference III	Conference IV	Conference V	Workshop I	Workshop II
5	7	11	1	3	9	25
6	8	12	2	4	24	26
15	14	17	10	21	42	27
16	20	18	13	22		
	29	23	19			
	35	34	28			
	36		30			
	37		31			
	38		32			
	39		33			
	40					
	41					

When all the children completed copying everything from the white board, one of the participants erased the board and prepared it for Assignment 5.

Assignment 5 – This time Shalom wrote down the names of the 9 Impressionists from Conference 4 and read out the two-line rhyming verses and the children had to name the Impressionist to which the lines belonged to. We again used the same method of going from youngest to oldest. Once this round was over, each one received the correct answers, printed out with the two sentences in black and the name of the Impressionist in red.

Following are the two-line verse and the correct replies:

1. Painting women was his delight
Using the brush strokes just right *(Pierre Auguste Renoir)*.

2. A genius who did not receive his due
Only after death his fame grew *(Paul Cezanne)*.

3. An artist who began a new style (impression) that has grown
Even today it is loved and well known *(Claude Monet)*.

4. A name that was almost the same
As the artist who then had much less fame *(Edouard Manet)*.

5. Dancers were his favorite subjects
But he also painted many other objects *(Edgar Degas)*.

6. Always helping a friend in need
He was a good friend indeed *(Frederic Bazille)*.

7. One woman among the nine
Whose paintings were so fine *(Berthe Morisot)*.

8. One Jew among the group
Who too was a good painter of this small troop. *(Camille Pissarro)*.

9. One of the richest of the new trend
Died penniless at the end *(Alfred Sisley)*.

Assignment 6 – based on Conference 5, choose 1 word or phrase associated with the scientist from the list below:

- Albert Einstein
- Galileo Galilei
- Sir Isaac Newton
- Leonardo da Vinci
- Theodor Maiman
- Charles Darwin
- Louis Pasteur
- Wilhelm Roentgen
- Benjamin Franklin

List of Words

Telescope, apple, kite, laser, X-ray, Beagle, relativity, radiation, pendulum, human body, differential calculus, bacteria, First Nobel Prize in Physics, photons, monkey, and yet it moves, vaccination, a scheme for flying, prism, ruby laser, electricity, an illustration of the bones of the hand, eye glasses, chickens, evolution, music lover especially violin.

The children did this exercise well. Most of the children remembered the facts from conference 5, a year ago.

Next on the agenda was painting; the activity that they all loved to do together. This time each one received an individual, very, small puzzle and painted the pieces of his own choice. This activity was followed by a nice, rewarding lunch.

Yaffa

<u>The First Three Assignments:</u>

As you recall, each participant had to choose 3 names from a list of 23 words. Then you had to send two names to two other participants with a copy to me. The third name you left for yourself. Now we will play a game in pantomime based on the third name that only one of you and I know who that person is. Everyone else will have to guess.

Each one tried to portray the person that he was presenting. We laughed a lot as each one tried to do a good theatrical presentation.

We then played a memory game with one of the sets of the

wooden blocks. Then we put on some music and danced, just for the exercise.

And finally came the big surprise of all, the one that the children had been waiting for so eagerly, our latest purchase in Madrid. We brought out the big package; it was huge. I am sure that you too are anxious so we will not keep you in suspense any longer. It was a floor piano; when we unwrapped it, the children became so excited. We let them all have a go at it; one at a time and sometimes two or three. Then we brought out the other big games and while they played, Shalom helped me set the tables for supper.

The parents arrived shortly. They too were surprised to see the big floor piano. We all partook of a nice supper; the children told them excitedly about the nice day; we gave them some souvenirs to take home together with their other supplies. They all left happily and Shalom and I felt so proud. It had been almost a full day of learning; to quote the children again, "It is so good to learn while having fun."

WORKSHOP IV

FUN WITH COUSINS FROM TORONTO IN HEBREW AND IN ENGLISH

30.6.2012

THE REASON that we had Workshop 4 three months following Workshop 3 was that my niece Judy, her husband Gadi and their three children Samantha 13, Aaron 10 and Jesse 7 were visiting from Toronto. It was the children's first visit to Israel. Most of their days were spent touring our beautiful country. We decided to give the parents a break one Saturday and have a Workshop for the 13 youngsters; 10 Israeli participants (Alon aged 5 now joined us) and the 3 Canadians. The problem was that we had a range of ages and a serious communication problem; the participants from Canada spoke very little Hebrew while most of our Israeli delegation knew little English. We needed a program that would be adaptable to all.

To make the day more enjoyable I prepared tasty meals suited to all palates as well as many good snacks.

Following is the Program

11:00-11:30 Around the table with a fresh bagel and chocolate milk

11:30-11:45 Jokes in English and Hebrew

11:45-13:00 Painting three, 9-piece puzzles

13:00-14:00 Card games in English and Hebrew

14:00-15:00 A break for lunch

15:00-16:00 The animal game in pantomime

16:00-16:30 Fruit and vegetable break while listening to my short story in two languages that I had written a few years before and that my friend Edna from the Weizmann Institute of Science had translated into Hebrew, "A Fruit or a Vegetable Children?"

16:30-18:00 Stories from the Bible in pantomime

18:00-19:00 Discussions of the day while partaking of goodies

Following our short refreshments, we all went into the living room and Shalom told a few jokes in Hebrew and English to start the day off with smiles. Then we went on to our first assignment:

Each participant received two pieces (some 3 pieces) of a 9-piece puzzle to paint. In all they were supposed to complete three puzzles that would be souvenirs for the three Canadian participants to take home with them. They worked nicely together; there were no language difficulties in this activity. In the end, everyone was pleased with his individual achievement. When all the pieces were done, they were put on the tray to dry.

We then had a language memory game that Shalom had prepared in his perfectly clear handwriting. There were 24 cards in all: 12 in English and 12 in Hebrew. They had to match the English word to the Hebrew one. The children were paired off as follows:

Shani and Jesse, Ido and Roni, Tamir and Samantha, Dotan with Maya and Alon, Shira and Ori, Eran with Aaron; working in pairs made the assignment more fun and there was a lot of laughter.

A nice lively lunch was followed by what we called the animal game which went like this: The children had to think of an animal and play it out in pantomime. These are the animals that the children chose: fish, butterfly, beetle, cow, bear, dog, elephant, penguin, lamb, dolphin, dove, octopus, turtle, and dinosaur. When an Israeli participant was chosen, the Canadian participants had to guess the animal and say it in English. When it was the Canadian participant's turn, only the Israeli participants could guess. We used our famous white board where Shalom wrote down the words in two columns, one in English and one in Hebrew. Here again we had fun learning the names in both languages.

The hard work called for a snack. I put out some fresh cut up fruit and vegetables to nibble on while I read out my story "A Fruit or a Vegetable Children" in English and then Shalom read my friend's (Edna Maayan) translation in Hebrew.

A Fruit or a Vegetable Children?

Yaffa Eliezer, Rehovot, July 2007

The vegetable and fruit communities were concerned! The children were not eating enough fruit and vegetables. Their diet was crammed with junk food and too many sweets. The dentists were complaining about cavities; the doctors were concerned about the growth in obesity. The children were not getting enough vitamins and minerals. Something had to be done before it was too late.

The vegetables and fruit took it upon themselves to help the children. They called an emergency meeting to declare war on junk food and sweets. They met in the supermarket after the workers had long gone home. There was a lot of noise and racket; everyone spoke at the same time.

"Quiet! You are screeching like a bunch of hens", yelled vegetable cabbage.

Orange rolled off the stall and asked for permission to speak.

"Orange juice is rich in vitamin C. It should be the first fruit on the list."

Apple jumped off the stall and pushed orange aside.

"Apple juice is better. Remember, an apple a day keeps the doctor away."

Grapes dropped to the ground.

"That's so old fashioned. Today children like to drink grape juice."

A chorus was heard in the background: "Mango juice, pineapple juice, banana and strawberry juice, pomegranate juice."

The stall with the vegetables began to shake with impatience.

"Juice, juice, juice. Enough with the juice. Children must learn to eat healthy vegetables and fruit. Tomato juice is very good for the children, but do you hear me roaring about tomato juice?" asked vegetable tomato annoyed. "Children must eat vegetables and fruit every day if they want to grow to be strong and healthy."

"Spinach is packed with iron; iron will make the children strong," put in vegetable spinach.

"I can become the children's favorite," said vegetable carrot. "Children love the color orange; besides, carrots taste good raw, cooked or juiced."

"Will you stop it with the juice already! Children have healthy teeth. They need to use them to chew," said vegetable broccoli annoyed.

Everyone began to speak at the same time. Again, there was a lot of noise and commotion.

"Quiet, stop your silly arguments. We know that we are all healthier than most of the other things that children eat today," said vegetable lettuce. "It does not matter if the children drink juice or chew the food. They must learn to eat lots of fruit and vegetables. The question is how can we make the children understand this."

"What can we do?" asked pear.

"We must do something to help them before it's too late," put in vegetable cucumber.

"I know", said spinach excitedly. "We can advertise our importance on google."

"Google! Hello, we are talking about children. Have you forgotten?" asked banana. Most children liked this fruit so that banana was looked upon as an authority on the topic of child behavior.

"Who do you think google all the time? This is the 21st century, remember. Children know more about the internet than most adults," said spinach. "Their parents put them in front of the screen before they are able to speak, and you know that it doesn't take long before they can teach the parents a thing or two about this new era."

"I think it's an excellent idea to use the internet," said vegetable corn. "We'll use Photoshop and make the pictures attractive."

"We can also use some good rhyming verses; children love rhyming verses."

Again, there was a lot of commotion. Each fruit and vegetable tried to make up a rhyme to show his importance.

"Stop bickering. Children are very smart and as soon as they realize how healthy we are, they will learn to include all of us in their diet. Okay, so we'll make up nice rhymes and have our pictures on the screen but it's still not enough to catch their interest. We must think of something more," said vegetable corn.

It became very quiet. Everybody put on their thinking caps. What could they do? Suddenly spinach spoke.

"I think I have found the perfect solution," said spinach. Everyone looked at spinach with disrespect. After all, children did not like spinach. They all began to speak at once.

Spinach ignored everyone's sneers and continued.

"We will offer the children a site on the web. We will make new fruit and vegetable pets and soon they will be sold everywhere. The parents will cooperate and will be happy to buy these pets for the children. The website will also offer games, prizes, stories and even recipes so that the parents will be interested and become involved. Every time the children begin eating a new vegetable or fruit the parents will sign in and the children will earn points. The more they eat the more points they will get; children love to play games and win points. The more fruit and vegetables they eat, the more their taste buds become adjusted to the taste and soon most of their diet will consist of fruits and vegetables." Everyone looked at spinach with new respect.

"That's a wonderful idea!" they all shouted together.

"But if we want our idea to succeed, we must include ice cream and chocolate," added spinach. "You see, if we advertise only food that children don't like they won't cooperate with us."

"For a minute you had me fooled," said peach. "You're an idiot after all. We're supposed to advertise fruits and vegetables; food that will make the children healthy, not sweets and junk food."

"Don't you understand? If we include chocolate and ice

cream, we will have their attention", said spinach determined not to be beaten.

"I agree with vegetable spinach," put in vegetable broccoli. "I even have a rhyme; a little bit of chocolate as a treat, can make each day very sweet."

"And I have one for ice cream," volunteered vegetable potato. "Ice cream on a hot day, chases the heat away."

"I see it this way; if they eat every day lots of fruit and vegetables, some ice cream and chocolate can't hurt them."

Everyone was looking at spinach who now had their attention. The fruit and vegetables all came to the same conclusion: vegetable spinach was not stupid after all. As a matter of fact, spinach was very clever and healthy.

The meeting was concluded. It was unanimously decided: If the children eat vegetables and fruit every day; some chocolates and ice cream are still okay!

The children enjoyed the story so much that by the time we finished reading it in English and Hebrew, we noticed that all the cut-up fruit and vegetables on the table were gone.

The time had come for the main event that Shalom had spent time preparing: Stories from the Bible. These were done in pantomime; some of them were hilarious.

Following are the different scenes and the characters:

<u>Act I</u>

Abraham (Eran), Sarah (Maya) and Isaac (Dotan)

Scene 1 – The sacrifice of Isaac

Scene 2 – The expulsion of Ishmael

Act II

Eliezer and Isaac (Dotan), Rebecca (Roni) and Jacob (Ido)

Scene 1- Eliezer looks for a bride for Isaac

Scene 2- Isaac meets Rebecca

Scene 3- Rebecca tells Jacob to steal the seniority

Act III

Jacob (Ido), Rachel (Shira) and Joseph (Jesse)

Scene 1- Jacob works 7 years to marry Rachel

Scene 2-Jacob and Rachel plan the escape

Scene 3-Joseph the favorite son

Act IV

Moses (Ori), Aaron, brother of Moses (Aaron) and Miriam, sister of Moses (Shani)

Scene 1-Moses in the ark

Scene 2-Exodus from Egypt

Scene 3-Moses brings the 10 Commandments

Act V

David (Tamir), Bat-Sheba (Samantha) and Solomon (Alon)

Scene 1-David sees Bat-Sheba

Scene 2-David escapes from Absalom

Scene3-David is old, and he decides that Solomon will be the next king

Following this fun activity, the children gathered around the table to partake of some snacks and we summarized the enjoyable day.

The parents arrived shortly to take the children home. The Toronto guests went to sleep at one of our children's home. We received hugs from all of them; we were happy that they had had a good time.

Beside the three beautiful puzzles that they all made together for the Canadian participants to take home, all the participants took their towels, the nice hats that we had bought especially for this workshop and some other small souvenirs.

A few days later when our guests came to say goodbye before they returned to Canada, I asked Jesse what the highlight of this trip was; he said, "The Workshop."

A week later

A week after our visitors left, I received a phone call from my niece Judy. She called to thank us for helping make their visit so unique, especially the workshop that the children continue to talk about. They enjoyed it very much. She also told me that Aaron was upset because he lost the hat that he had received at the workshop. Although he has many hats, he was upset because it was such a good souvenir. I told her that I would go back to the store where I had bought the hats and buy another one. The next day I went back to the store, but they did not have any hats left in that style. When I told this story to my daughter, she immediately told her son Dotan and he offered to give Aaron his hat.

The following day, I mailed Dotan's hat to Aaron.

WORKSHOP V

SCIENCE AND ART

20.3.2013

Workshop 5 was based mainly on two topics:

Science

To continue the discussion with the children about the famous 9 scientists introduced in Conference 5 and reviewed in Workshop 3 and to widen and extend their knowledge about these men's important contribution to mankind.

Art

The painting of a 9-piece puzzle by each participant to take home. This idea came to me following Workshop 4 when we did three, 9-piece puzzles for our Canadian participants to take home. To make this even more special this time, I bought gouache paints and different sized brushes.

We began the day as usual with chocolate milk and rolls. Throughout the day they partook of good snacks. We had one of their favorite lunches. We watched films with popcorn; played memory games with our house produced wooden blocks as well as other games.

The name of Shalom's talk this time was "The Scientists in the last 500 years and how they became famous? For his lecture, he used the white board. The names of the 9 scientists from Conference 5 were listed in columns and he asked the children the following:

To choose the scientist of his or her choice; name at least one important thing that he or she remembered related to him. Naturally, they all chose the scientists that they had portrayed in the play in Conference 5:

Eran
Galileo: I think that he is remembered mostly for the telescope.

Shira
Newton: Is most known for the laws of gravitation and associated with the story of the apple that fell off the tree.

Tamir

Darwin: Is remembered mainly for the gigantic turtle. I also remember the name of his boat the Beagle because it reminds of the word bagel that I love to eat.

Roni

Leonardo da Vinci: Is most famous for his painting of the Mona Lisa.

Maya

Roentgen: I remember the story of the image of his and his wife's bones which led him to discover the X-ray.

Ori

Einstein: I remember his equation $E=mc^2$.

Ido

Louis Pasteur: Is remembered for his experiment with the chickens, which led to his development of the vaccine.

Dotan

Theodore Maiman: His outstanding contribution was the building of the first laser in 1960.

Shani

Benjamin Franklin: Franklin's kite experiments during thunderstorms inspired him to initiate the search for electricity.

After the first round, Shalom gave them the opportunity to add more facts that they remembered about these nine, not only about those that they had portrayed but about all nine of them. These were the additions that Shalom included on the board for each person:

Galileo Galilei, the language of science is mathematics, the mechanical law for motion, the pendulum law, measuring time with human pulse.

Isaac Newton, laws of motion, new mathematics, President of Royal Society.

Charles Darwin, science of evolution, all species of life descended from a common predecessor, father of modern biology.

Leonardo da Vinci described and accurately painted the human body (external and internal), a great engineer who designed a human flying, a submarine, a tank, a gun, a bridge, drainage canal system and a harp.

Wilhelm Roentgen, First Nobel prize in physics.

Albert Einstein, general relativity, the photon, a pioneer of quantum mechanics, Nobel Prize for the photon.

Louis Pasteur, the father of medical microbiology, pasteurization, developed vaccines against chicken cholera. anthrax, and rabies, received the highest decoration "Legion of Honor".

Theodore Maiman, a physicist and an engineer who received many awards and recognitions after he built the first laser in 1960.

Benjamin Franklin, one of the founding fathers of the United States Constitution, his head is on the USA 100$, research on electricity, inventor of bi-focal lenses, kite experiments during thunderstorms.

The children had a lot of fun and were excited at how much they remembered. The white board filled up quickly with the information.

The art project was carried out in a much quieter and more relaxed atmosphere. There was no excitement here, but they were happy; some were humming while producing their individual pieces for the puzzle. By using the brush strokes they produced amazing artwork.

Following our art project, we had a good snack, played some games, and then went back to the table to have "Around the Table Discussion" which this time we taped.

Shalom

Do you think that we should hold another conference in the coming summer, or should we continue with the workshops?

Eran

I think that all our meetings are fun and the learning sessions that you both prepare are very important for us. It is a good idea that during the summer vacation when we are away from school, we can continue to learn. In general, you always manage to set up many nonstop, various activities and we are busy all the time. This shows how much thought you invest in each detail. All the different activities, all the sweets, everything is great.

Maya

To start with, it is very nice to be together with all the cousins, especially during the summer vacation when we have so much time. We learn together and play together and partake of all the challenging things that you prepare. You always plan every detail so that we could enjoy ourselves and have a good time. Thank you for everything that you do for us.

Ido

I think that the conferences are a lot of fun. I do not know anyone in the world who does these things with their grandchildren; all this planning and preparing and everything turns out so successful. It unifies the families. It is not like learning in school. Here we are learning in a good atmosphere, while having a lot of fun. With each conference the standards are higher and more challenging. And one more thing, to wake up in the morning together with everyone is so enjoyable and relaxing. It is great.

Ori

If we would enjoy 20% of the things that we learn in school like we do here, then we would enjoy school much more and be much better students. Here we learn in a different atmosphere, with many pleasant experiences. In school we never do things like we do here; maybe 20% of the artwork, but nothing more. In short, school is not great.

Dotan

I have many things to say. The first thing is about the learning. I never felt before that I enjoy learning. I do enjoy it here. One time we studied a similar topic in school, and I felt so good that I remembered it from one of the conferences. Then I thought of something. What will happen if you decide not to make any more sleepover conferences? Gili and Alon have not yet attended a conference so I thought maybe we could suggest to one of the parents to do it. And then I said to myself, I cannot see it. Nobody will do it.

Shira

For one, the learning here is totally different from school. And we really appreciate it. It is wonderful to get together during the summer vacation and be here for two whole days. It really unifies us together and it is fun to study here.

Roni

In my opinion it is important to have another conference. We like to get together here. It is a lot fun.

Tamir

We must have another conference because we always have a good time here. I think maybe you also enjoy it because it makes us appreciate you more.

Dotan

What do you mean it makes us appreciate them more?

Tamir

I did not mean that. I only wanted to say that we all feel closer. Also, from the point of view of learning, you introduce a lot of general knowledge which is very useful for us. The atmosphere here is great and it is wonderful to wake up in the morning with all the cousins, get pampered all the time and all the wonderful souvenirs that you find for us. All the fun things we do here and being together is great. Especially, the fact that Maya and I live far from here and we do not always have a chance to get together. And if you were to make a children camp, it would be the best camp in the world.

At this point Dotan raised his hand he wanted to add something.

Dotan

Here we are close in age and we are not only cousins but also friends. These conferences bring us cousins even closer to one another.

Then Maya raised her hand:

Maya

I want to add something. I have to say again how wonderful it is here. It is great!

Then Eran raised is hand:

Eran

When you are both in Madrid, instead of enjoying yourselves and going to see different places, you are always planning the conferences and running around buying special souvenirs and we really appreciate this. Everybody applauded and said that they agreed.

Shani

It is really a lot of fun. All the cousins meet and do things together. Like Dotan said, we are close in age and we are not only cousins; we are all good friends. Every time we learn a lot and there is always something new in the artwork activities. I hope that there will be another conference (and then she crossed her fingers and continued). When Saba and Safta will see this recording of 11 minutes and realize how we are all excited and anxious to have another conference, then they will decide to have one.

Shalom summarized this little discussion around the table by quoting the great Roman leader Julius Cesar who said, "I came, I saw, I conquered (veni, vidi, vici)".

Following our stimulating and heart-warming discussion the children continued with the games while we waited for their parents to arrive and join us for a light meal.

CONFERENCE VI

A TOUCH OF ITALY DAY ONE, LAUGHTER DAY TWO

August 8-9, 2014

August 2011

I BEGAN STUDYING ITALIAN, in Tel Aviv, sponsored by the Italian Embassy a couple of years ago and I was anxious to return to Rome. To my delight, Shalom was invited to Scotland to teach at the Summer school and on the way back, we stopped in Rome, for one week.

Rome has always been one of my favorite cities in Europe. Shalom and I have visited this city several times and had spent two months in Frascati where Shalom and his colleague had worked together to organize a week long conference in Rome. During that time, we visited Rome many times.

It was while we were in Rome following Scotland that I told Shalom that our next conference should be on Italy. He thought it was a great idea and during this visit, besides purchasing some Italian books for me to read, we also bought hats, pens, pencils as well as beautiful magnets featuring masks from the Venice Festivals for the grandchildren. Then on the last day, we found a wonderful little book featuring the attractions of ancient Rome today and showed how they were when they were constructed. The book also included a DVD about Rome.

Now three years following Conference 5, we are finally having Conference 6. During the three-year gap, we held three one day workshops.

Today, there was still a gap between the older participants and their two younger cousins Alon and Gili. Still, in the end, everyone walked away happy, profitable and smiling. How did we do it?

Preparations

This summer I had registered for an Italian Conversation Course in Tel Aviv. By now, I had done quite a few courses, and this was a good opportunity to practice what I had learned so far. The grandchildren were involved as usual with many activities and family trips. Thus, to coordinate a suitable date was more difficult than in the past. I persuaded Shani to do it this time.

As in the past, we purchased pajamas, bath towels and hand towels; this time 11. We also bought 11 white t-shirts and two more water bottles and toothbrushes for Alon and Gili. I also replenished my supplies of pencils, erasers, sharpeners, markers and games.

I was busy shopping, cooking and during it all, missiles were being launched into Israel, first into the south and soon into the rest of the country. The TV was constantly on when I was in the kitchen preparing the meals for the conference. What began on the 7th of July and called an operation, soon turned into a full-scale war, and lasted almost 7 weeks. In the past most of the missile attacks had lasted no more than two weeks. Shalom and I were sure that this latest round of hostilities would end by the time that our conference would take place, but we were wrong. We discussed cancelling the conference a couple of times, but the children had waited so long for another conference that in the end, with the support of their parents, we decided to go ahead with it.

Today, in every modern building in Israel, a safe room is mandatory. The safe room is constructed of reinforced concrete, a heavy sealed window and a steel vault like door. At the sound of the siren everyone rushes into the room, closes the heavy sealed window and door, and waits for the clear signal. In the older structures, where there are no safe rooms, people must take cover in the stairway.

Our apartment is equipped with a safe room where we have a TV and a divan. This is the grandchildren's room all year round used as the guest room, the playroom etc. Our worry was that the siren would go off when one of them was upstairs, under the shower, but we risked it.

Before the conference, as usual, Shalom took the whole

week off because he had a lot of work to do: labeling the towels, pajamas and t-shirts; printing, cutting, gluing, preparing his lectures etc. We were so busy that we spent less time in front of the TV than we usually do during such difficult times. We were lucky that between the 5th to the 18th of August there was a temporary cease fire. Although some missiles were still being fired into Israel, they were mainly fired at the border.

Some of the parents sent mattresses; all of them sent sheets, pillows and blankets that were dropped off the day before by some of them. The night before the conference, we relaxed in front of the television with a good movie.

DAY ONE

We woke up early and made the last-minute preparations. Shalom went to buy a challah, some Danish pastry and croissants.

By 10 a.m., our 9 older participants arrived: excited and happy. All the bags were put away. We handed out the hand towels; each one with his or her name inscribed on the towel as in the past. The girls hung theirs up in one bathroom while the boys hung theirs in the other one. Then we took our places at the two tables.

The scenes facing them were Italian: a beautiful, big, colorful map, depicting some monuments with emphasis on famous spots to visit were highlighted. We had received this big map from the Italian Embassy in Tel Aviv a few years ago. I also put up three beautiful aprons with Italian scenery and a beautiful sun umbrella with lively colors and scenes; all purchased in Rome on our last visit more than three years ago. Italian songs filled the room from a CD that I had especially bought for this day.

The children enjoyed the croissants and drank the chocolate milk together with Shalom. As soon as everyone finished eating, I cleared the table and we started the day with a small lecture that Shalom had prepared about the history of Italy. He used the beautiful map to point out the different regions and explained how they were created to become one nation. The children were very attentive and listened quietly.

Following his short and interesting lecture, we went into the living room to see the sites of Rome in the book featuring the attractions of ancient Rome today and how they were when they had been constructed. The book was passed from participant to participant.

Then we put on the CD that was inside the book and watched a movie about Rome. To make the viewing more interesting for them, we held a competition between the boys and the girls. Each one took his notebook and pencil and wrote down the sites from the CD. When the film came to an end, the girls went into the grandchildren's room while the boys stayed in the living room. The girls merged their list into one. The boys did the same and what excitement followed as we checked off the sites. It was a tie! This put everyone in a very good mood for the next attraction: another competition.

Shalom and I had prepared cards with famous Italian personalities that we had printed out from the computer. Shalom had cut the pictures into passport size and glued them onto the blank side of the playing cards that I had bought at a hobby store. Each set consisted of three cards with the name and photo of the well-known Italian personalities and only one included the period that he lived. For example, there was the opera singer Luciano Pavarotti, the explorers Christopher Columbus and Marco Polo, the physicists Galileo Galilei and Enrico Fermi, the musical composer Antonio Vivaldi, the poet Dante Alighieri, the Roman general and statesman Julius Caesar, The painters Rafael Sanzio, Sandro Botticelli, Michelangelo and Leonardo da Vinci, and few other famous personalities.

The cards were placed upside down on the table. The object of the game was to find the three identical photos, including the one with the period that he lived. There was noise and excitement during the game.

Then they all went to wash their hands and some of them helped me set up the table for lunch. We had minestrone soup, followed by spaghetti with a mild tomato sauce and some fresh vegetables. Dessert was dairy so we had a rich quality ice cream with chocolate trimming, Italian biscuits, and some fruit.

With our palates satisfied, we were in a mood to get back to work; it was time for our 36-piece puzzle. Each child received 4 pieces to try and copy the beautiful Venetian masks on the magnets that we had bought in Rome. Once they were all done, the pieces were put on the tray to dry.

They washed their hands again and then we all went into the living room. I handed each participant a sheet of paper with a few simple words in Italian such as si, no, grazie, buongiorno, arrivederci, etc. and the numbers 1 to 10. They tried to learn some of the vocabulary, the numbers and tried to repeat the words to one another.

I also gave them another sheet of paper with the words to an Italian song "Arrivederci Roma" in English. Then they received the hats that we had purchased in Rome and we all tried to sing the song Arrivederci Roma in English, along with the CD in Italian.

While waiting for Gili and Alon to arrive we spoke about the day. As soon as they came, we put on a short funny movie.

The children then drew numbers for who would shower first while the rest continued to watch the movie. Alon and Gili were the only ones who watched the movie from beginning to the end because they had taken their showers at home. When everyone was washed and ready, Alon and Gili changed into their new pajamas and we took some group photos, one on the stairs and one on the couch in the living room.

Since it was Friday, we gathered around the big table in the dining room. Shalom made the Shabbat (Kiddush) prayer and we had some wine; the participants had grape juice.

The Shabbat Dinner included chicken soup with noodles, sweet chicken in the oven, corn on the cob, roasted potatoes and a vegetable salad. For dessert we had some fruit with non-dairy ice cream.

As soon as we were able to move again, some children helped me clear the table while others brushed their teeth. Once everyone was ready, the children helped arrange their sleeping quarters. Those who were tired went to their beds, others went upstairs to talk, while others watched TV.

Shalom and I were so exhausted that as soon as Alon and Gili were fast asleep, we too went to bed, leaving the older ones to tend for themselves.

DAY TWO

We wanted all the children to have breakfast together because we had a surprise for them. Some of them woke up early on their own while others needed our coaxing.

This time we had breakfast in the dining room. The menu included three different kinds of serial and slices of Challah dipped in egg, fried and served with maple syrup. So, what was the surprise that awaited them? Each participant received a beautiful glass bowl with a colored rim and a matching transparent tablespoon with the same color as the rim of the bowl. The new participants were the first to choose the color. The last bowl that remained was for Shalom. At the end of the conference the children took the bowls and spoons home, along with all their other bonuses; some of the children are still using the bowls today when they have serial at home.

Following our satisfying breakfast, the children brushed their teeth and got dressed. We put away the mattresses and folded up the sheets and then we all went into the living room to begin our day of laughter

The first item on the agenda was my presentation *"Laughter is the Best Medicine"*.

Yaffa

The more you laugh the better you feel but be careful not to cross the red line. At times you laugh so hard that it is hard to stop. It is dangerous to exaggerate in anything you do even good things. Know when to stop. Laugh for pleasure but stay in control.

Laughter makes you forget bad things and chases away bad thoughts. Laughter is contagious; it is like a chain reaction. One person begins to laugh, this makes the other person laugh, and the other and before long there is a roomful of people laughing.

You can laugh at anything and everything and it always makes you feel good. You do not need a reason to laugh. It is fun to laugh with company, but you can also laugh alone. Just stand in front of the mirror and make funny faces at yourself and before long, you will be laughing.

Laughter is a good exercise for the face. You move the facial muscles, and this makes your face look younger and your skin more radiant.

Laughing is a good way to start the day. If you laugh in the morning, you will laugh all day.

When you laugh with people you love, this is the best laughter of all. It puts everyone into a great mood. Today we will make this day full of laughter and fun to bring out the best in all of us.

In short, laughter makes us happy, pleasant and cheerful. This is our theme for today. So, let me see you all smiling.

Soon everyone was smiling. And then Shalom took over and told them some funny jokes and everyone was laughing and laughing and laughing.

Then we brought out the bag with the white t-shirts. Each one had his name inscribed on the back. We handed out the special markers to be used on the t-shirts to create designs.

Some copied the designs that I had printed out from the computer while others did their own original creations; all the time talking, singing and laughing.

As soon as a t-shirt was completed, it was turned inside out and Shalom steamed it so that the design would be preserved. Then each one put on his new t-shirt and had his picture taken. Attired in the new t-shirts, we took group photos and then they all went into the living room and watched a very funny movie with popcorn.

Following the movie, we set up all the games and while everyone was busy playing, Shalom and I began to get their lunch ready.

Right after lunch, it was time for our play. This time Shalom had printed out the text in big bold letters so that the children would be able to read their lines from a distance. He affixed these typed pages onto Bristol paper, and these were then placed on the stand (on the artist easel) when needed. Each participant's part was highlighted. Shalom was in charge of changeing the pages.

This time the play was entitled" To Laugh at Nothing at All." My aim was to get the children in a good mood; to fuse together the big and small and most of all to make them all laugh at nothing at all. It was similar in thought to Shakespeare's Much Ado About Nothing but, of course, a lot sillier. It was an amateur and unsophisticated one act play written for a mixed age group of children.

The play began with Dotan who commanded Ori to laugh. Ori was surprised and asked why he should laugh; to which Dotan replied that he was in charge to make everyone laugh and that he was merely carrying out my request. And so, it follows that Ori tells Eran to laugh, who tells Roni who tells Maya and all the rest of the participants.

I wrote some humorous lines in between to make it funny and to cause the children to laugh because not everyone was ready to laugh at nothing at all. Dotan had no problem laughing and at times became so hysterically drunk with laughter, that he had to leave the scene to get himself sober. Shani was the last one to come forward. She tried to analyze and find the logic behind the reason why I wanted them to laugh. She explained it the Shani way and finally it made sense to everyone and so they all began to laugh and laugh and laugh.

Although Gili and Alon did not participate in the play because the text was too difficult for them to read, they were the audience and laughed the most.

Everyone was in a great mood and became even happier when we told them that next on the agenda was the bazaar. We have mentioned the bazaars throughout the book and how and when we began having them, why the children look forward to them so much, but we have never described the hours of shopping and tedious work behind it. We have therefore dedicated this time a whole chapter for the bazaar.

THE BAZAAR

Putting together a Bazaar is no simple task. First, you must check your closet to see what things the children would like to take home (the ones in perfect condition of course). Then you must prepare a list of items to buy for the bazaar; go look for interesting things to add. When you are abroad and you have hours to spend, you can really find interesting items like I did in Madrid.

And sometimes, opportunities arise. Take this conference for instance. The FIFA World Cup finals took place in Brazil from the 12th of June to the 13th of July 2014. McDonald's was one of the FIFA World Cup sponsors and they sold authentic soccer balls, like the ones used at the games. How could we not buy two balls for our bazaar? Then one day I was out grocery shopping and I saw a practical big travelling bag in the window shop at one of the stores. Immediately I bought two.

When I was finally satisfied that we had enough items for sale, we first had to decide how much to price each item.

Then it was Shalom who took over.

He had to do the following:

How much (monopoly) money should each participant receive?

How should he distribute the bills to have enough change when a big currency is used?

Put a tag on each item.

Add up the total and so on. During the Bazaar, if there is

one item that more than one participant wants, then we have an auction and the highest bidder buys the item.

This year he omitted the bills of 2 to make the math easier for the younger participants. Shalom placed different color stickers on the items: for 1 shekel = green, 10 shekels =yellow, 20 shekels=blue and 50 shekels= red.

What items were for sale at this year's Bazaar?

50 shekels: 2 footballs, 2 travel bags, 1 necklace, 1 special game called Goblet, by the well-known company Fox mind.
(subtotal = 300 shekel)

20 shekels: 1 used box of Lego blocks, 1 pack of special playing cards, 3 DVDs, 1 book, 1 special set FCB (Football Club Barcelona), 1 special key chain, 1 bracelet, 4 box games.
(subtotal = 260 shekel)

10 shekels: 2 key chains, 1 fan, 3 bracelets, 2 pairs of earrings, 1 game Hangman, 2 change purses, 1 wooden doll, 2 alphabet telephone notebooks, 1 deck of cards, 6 card games, 5 writing blocks, 1 small bag, 1 notebook for fun activities, 2 workbooks about Italy for fun activities, 1 package of stickers, 2 small sew by number embroidery blocks.
(subtotal = 330 shekel)
1 shekel: 40 items
(subtotal = 40 shekel)
Total money = 1030 shekel

Each participant received 200 monopole bills: One bill of 100, one bill of 50, one bill of 20, one bill of 10, three bills of 5 and 5 bills of 1. Each participant received 200 shekels. (total received among all the participants = 2200 shekels). In this way there was enough money but not too much for the auction sales.

The Bazaar was successful! Everyone behaved in a grown-up manner. The auction sales were carried out in good behavior.

Shortly following the bazaar their parents arrived. We all had supper together which this year included pizza together with some dishes that I prepared.

Soon after supper, they collected the belongings and went home. This time they had a lot of packages that included: their blankets and pillows (some had mattresses as well), new pajamas; a bath towel; hand towels; new t-shirts; hats, pencil cases that included new pencils, pens, sharpeners, erasers etc.; glass bowls and tablespoons for eating serial; small jars containing jellybeans and others with m&m's and their purchases at the bazaar.

Gili and Alon received special gifts. The other nine participants received a disc on key with a small box for storage.

Everyone left happy with a big smile on their faces. We were happy that the conference had been a success and that no siren had disturbed our peace. On the 9th of August Israel was still at war that finally ended on August 26th.

After the conference we received calls from the participants thanking us and expressing how much they had enjoyed the conference. We could hear it in their voices how happy, sincere, and excited they all were.

We also received two letters (in Hebrew of course) that we have translated as best as we could to give them the right meaning that they deserve and to do justice to what the young authors wanted to express at the time.

From Maya, (age 11 ½)

How are you Safta?

I would like to thank you and Saba very, very much for all the planning and the time invested. We can imagine how much time you had spent.

It was a very successful conference. The themes on Italy and Rome were very interesting and we came away learning a lot.

Yesterday, on the way home, Tamir and I told our parents about the conference, and I realized how many important Italian names and places that I remembered from the documentary that we saw and from the memory game that we played.

The second day of the conference was "the day for laughter," where we all relaxed, enjoyed, and laughed a lot. It was a less serious day and very suitable for Alon and Gili. Alon, and I am sure that also Gili, enjoyed their first conference very much.

So, we want to thank you again for all the planning, the thinking and all the time spent for this conference.

And I can speak on behalf of all the grandchildren that this conference was great, successful and we REALLY enjoyed it.

So, thank you very much and love you a lot (emoji of a heart).

From Shani, age (16 ½)

Dearest Safta and Saba

We arrived home not long ago tired but very pleased (emoji of a happy face).

I just wanted to tell you thanks, thank you for all that you are doing for us; to thank you for all the shopping sprees, your thoughts and the many efforts that we know that are required for what we call "Grandchildren Conferences."

I am sure that you know, but even so it is worthwhile to repeat it again, how much everyone enjoys the different activities that you prepare for us and how pleasant it is for us to learn new things at the conferences.

In short, we would like to tell you how much we appreciate everything you do for us; we cannot think of other grandparents who would do something similar for their grandchildren. So, we salute you and are proud to call you our Safta and Saba.

Safta, thank you for all the delicious dishes that you cook for us, for your creativity, the plays that you prepare, the puzzles and all your original ideas that you come up with; things that other people would think are strange, you find the importance to include them because you are sure that we might enjoy them. In the end it turns out that you are right!

Saba, thank you for your planning and your thoughts that you invest in our conferences. Every second is plotted out in such detail that we use the time efficiently and enjoy ourselves while learning. Thank you for your readiness to teach us new subjects and to enlarge our general knowledge; we always learn something new from you.

Saba and Safta, thank you that you are who you are; making us laugh sometimes with your small disagreements; investing hours of thinking how to make things better and in short, you are the best saba and safta! (emoji of a heart).

I hope that you know how much we love you and if you do not then we want you to know that we love you the most in the world.

From us

Shani, Ido and Eran

THE PLAY

To Laugh at Nothing at All

Dotan and Ori, two of the participants, are just sitting around not doing anything.

Ori, you remember that Safta wants us all to laugh today.

To laugh at what?

Just laugh. It doesn't matter at what.

You must be joking. I should laugh just like that.

Yes, otherwise, I will tickle you.

Okay, I'll laugh. Ha, ha, ha

Eran walks in.

Ori why are you laughing?

I don't know. Dotan told me to laugh.

Dotan told you to laugh and you are laughing. Do you always do what Dotan tells you to do?

Dotan walks in.

Eran laugh.

Why?

Because Ori told you to laugh.

Not good enough.

Because I am telling you to laugh.

Still not good enough.

Safta wants us all to laugh today. She probably has a plan and she put me in charge to make sure that everyone laughs. So please laugh. That's good enough. Ha, ha, ha

Roni walks in.

Eran, what's so funny?

Nothing.

Then why are you laughing?

Ori told me to laugh because Dotan told him to laugh.

And you always do what Ori tells you to do.

Dotan walks in again.

Yes, Eran, you must do what Ori tells you to do because Ori must do what I tell him to do because the idea is Safta's. She wants everyone to laugh.

Okay, if Safta wants us to laugh, I will laugh, ha, ha, ha.

Maya walks in

Roni, what's so funny?

Nothing is funny.

So why are you laughing?

Because Eran told me to laugh.

Eran told you to laugh and that's why you are laughing.

Yes, and Eran is laughing because Ori told him to laugh, and Ori is laughing because Dotan told him to and it's all because Safta wants everyone to laugh.

Well, if Safta wants us to laugh then okay, ha, ha, ha

Shira walks in

What's so funny?

Nothing. Roni told me to laugh.

Why?

Because Eran told her to laugh and Ori told him to laugh and Dotan told Ori to laugh.

Wait a minute. If I understand correctly, Dotan told Ori to

laugh, Ori told Eran to laugh, Eran told Roni to laugh, and Roni told you to laugh. This is stupid.

Dotan who is still on stage gets closer to Shira.

Okay, start laughing.

Why should I laugh if nothing is funny?

Because I am telling you to.

But nothing is funny.

I know but Safta wants us all to laugh and put me in charge to make sure that everyone laughs.

But nothing is funny.

I'll tickle you.

Don't you dare.

Then laugh!

Okay, okay, ha, ha, ha

Tamir walks in

Shira, why are you pretending to laugh?

I'm not pretending, I am laughing. Ha, ha, ha

Okay, you are laughing, but why? What's so funny?

Nothing is funny. Maya told me to laugh and if I don't laugh Dotan is going to tickle me.

Okay, that makes sense. Why did Maya tell you to laugh?

Because Roni told her to laugh.

That makes even more sense. So why did Roni tell Maya to laugh.

Because Eran told her to laugh, and Ori told him to laugh and Dotan told Ori to laugh.

But why?

I don't know. Safta told Dotan to laugh and to make sure

that everyone laughs. Now if I don't laugh, Dotan will tickle me. And if you don't laugh, I will tickle you.

Go ahead. It doesn't bother me.

But Tamir, if you don't laugh, Dotan will tickle me. Come on, Tamir. You have a good heart, help me out.

Okay, ha, ha, ha

Ido walks in

Tamir, why are you laughing?

Shira told me to laugh

Why?

Because Maya told her to laugh.

And because Shira told you to laugh, you are laughing.

But don't you see, Roni told Maya to laugh because Eran told her to laugh because Ori told him to laugh because Dotan told Ori to laugh. Can't you just laugh?

No, not when nothing is funny. I don't understand why everyone is telling everyone to laugh. Has everyone declared today the day of laughter?

It's all Safta's idea. Don't ask me why, but she wants everyone to laugh so why not please her.

Okay, if you put it that way. Why didn't you say so in the beginning? You know that I always do what Safta wants me to do.

Shani is the last one to walk in.

Why is everyone laughing?

Ido is the first to speak.

It's a long story. Just join in the fun and laugh.

Just like that I should laugh.

It's Safta's idea. She told Dotan to be in charge and to make sure that everyone laughs so why not please her.

Did I say that I don't want to please her? But if she wants everyone to laugh, she must have a reason. Dotan, stop laughing for a minute I want to talk to you.

Dotan is holding his stomach. He cannot stop laughing.

Dotan, maybe I should bring you a book to read. When your mother was a child, she and Shira's mother got hysterical one day and couldn't stop laughing. Saba told her that he would bring her a book to read.

Now you're making me laugh even more.

Dotan please stop laughing for a minute and let's think why Safta wants us all to laugh.

Because she wants to invent a laughter day.

Very funny, Dotan.

No, I'm serious.

Safta says that it's better to laugh than to cry.

That's a good answer, Shira.

Because laughter puts everyone in a good mood.

Even better, Roni.

Because when we all laugh at nothing, we look funny and it makes everyone laugh, be happy and Gili and Alon could enjoy this play.

Close Maya, but not exactly.

Okay. So why did Safta tell me to make sure that everyone should laugh. I read that in his book of Oliver Twist, the famous British author who lived during the 19th century, Charles Dickens wrote that there is nothing more contagious than laughter. Maybe she wants to start a good contagious flu.

Very funny, Dotan. I read somewhere that Charlie Chaplin,

who was a famous movie star of the silent films, said that a day without laughter is a day wasted. So why did Safta write this play about laughter? Let's see, I think because laughter is a good thing. You don't need an excuse to laugh. Safta wanted to show us that you don't need to hear a good joke or see a funny movie to laugh. It's enough when people who really like one another, get together to play, paint, and listen to lectures are already happy and in a good mood. We are always happy to be together and maybe she wanted to write a nonserious play to put big smiles on our face and especially for Alon and Gili. So, all together now, let's Laugh at Nothing at All.

WORKSHOP VI

STRENGTH IN NUMBERS

15.10.2014

TODAY WE SERVED the children croissants with their chocolate milk like the ones that Shalom and I had in Paris. We spread out a big napkin from Café de Florc on the easel that we had saved from one of our trips. While the children and Shalom enjoyed their treat, I dived into my welcome speech.

Yaffa

"Welcome, I am so excited to get started. You know why? We are going to do a special art project. Sounds good? I know that you will like it.

During our recent trip to Madrid, while on one of my

walking outings, I walked into a store and my eyes landed on a box of colors that are used for painting on glass. You can imagine my excitement. Yes, I see your faces lighting up with excitement now; this is exactly how I felt.

The title of the workshop today is "Strength in Numbers" and Saba has prepared a very interesting lecture for you.

As usual, we have planned a full and exciting day with many activities, some more difficult than others. Help one another as you always do and by doing things together, we shall succeed in our missions. If you look at the white board, you will see the program for today: You are getting a notebook in the shape of a clock, marked with the different hours; please copy the program according to the time in the right place in the notebook. In addition, we have **six different task** stations: Everyone will receive a small bag containing a few items. At every station you will find everything necessary to fulfill your task. At the last station, number 6, you will find a big bag in which you will be able to store all your prizes and gifts to take home.

My welcome speech was followed by a lot of excitement. We were off to a good start! We cleared the table and Shalom presented the following talk on Darwin, one of our famous scientists of past encounters.

Shalom

Charles Robert Darwin who lived between 1809 –1882, was an English biologist, best known for his theory that all species of life have descended over time from a common ancestor. As I have told you in the past, the humans, you, your parents, Safta and I and the different species of monkeys have all developed from a previous primitive monkey.

The title of our workshop today is **Strength in Numbers**. What has this title to do with Darwin? I will give you the answer at the end of my 10-minute talk.

I am sure that most of you all remember **Charles Darwin**, one of our scientists from Conference 5 three years ago. Some of you may even remember everything that I am going to say today about Darwin's life. But I think that the nice bookmarks that we bought for you in Madrid, summarize the Darwin theory, namely, how men developed, in a popular and funny way. Therefore, I will now try, in an interesting way, to repeat what you already know.

Charles Darwin was born in 1809. As a young man he studied medicine, but he did not want to become a doctor. He therefore seized the opportunity to join the long, 5-year journey on a ship named The Beagle. During this journey on The Beagle, Darwin spent most of his free time on land, assembling natural history collections and summarizing everything in his notes. When the ship reached the isolated islands of Galapagos in the Pacific Ocean, Darwin found different types of birds from island to island. There he also found the big (turtle). The birds and animals were unlike any that he had seen in the South American continent located in the vicinity of the islands.

From his observations, Darwin concluded that all creatures developed in time according to the appropriate environments and only the fittest of them all survived. By the "fittest" Darwin did not mean the biggest or the strongest but the ones who could survive in the specific location where they lived. As you know, the big and strong dinosaurs disappeared when something happened on our planet and the environment changed drastically.

Today man rules our planet; it is man and not the strong lions or big elephants or monkeys or any other animal. Why? Because many years ago (a few hundred thousand years) when the human species developed (perhaps from some ancestor monkey) man had the ability to think, talk and communicate with one another on a large scale. This ability enabled the few wondering individuals to become a tribe. Later, a few tribes united to become a city (about 10 thousand years ago), and still later a few cities unified to become a country and some of them became big empires (like the Roman empire about 2 thousand years ago). All this because the power of two is bigger than that of one and the power of many is more than that of a few individuals. Man was able to think, to communicate on a variety of subjects, and this enabled him to form large groups and to rule the planet. As I said in the beginning **together** is always the best. I hope you enjoyed my small lecture.

We could see by the looks on the children's faces and their loud applause that they did and could have listened to more, but it was now time to try out the 6 stations:

Station 1:

11 small wine glasses, awaited the children's artistic designs along with different size paint brushes and the special box of paints used on glass. Following is the order at this station which

was determined by the number picked from the hat: Ori, Shira, Shani, Tamir, Eran, Maya, Roni, Dotan, Ido, Gili and Alon.

Station 2:

Gili and Alon begin a puzzle

Station 3:

each participant receives special markers to paint a reproduction of one of the photos of the Impressionists on a bookmark.

Station 4:

each one receives a postcard and a pen to write an imaginary meeting with one of the Italian personalities from Conference 6.

Station 5:

each one gets a small bag where inside is a small canvas with one special marker that is made up of smaller markers, each one a different shade.

Station 6:

relaxing center with games.

Once each participant had his turn at all the stations, we put on a short play in pantomime about a family of five and a maid,

A Comical Satire

The actors: Dotan, the father; Shani, the mother; Tamir, the maid; Eran, the son; Ido, the son; Ori (with one of my hats), the daughter.

Following is the story:

The family is sitting around the table, having breakfast together. The children are home from school. The father, who is absent-minded, is making the last-minute preparations to go to work. Every time he forgets to take something with him. The mother is anxious for him to leave. She has planned the day with the children. The maid wants everyone to leave so she could clean the house and take a nap.

The father takes his hat, plants a small kiss on each child's cheek, a bigger one for his wife and almost wants to kiss the cleaning lady but stops and leaves. Everyone is happy. The mother starts planning the day ahead; the maid begins to clean when suddenly the bell rings. She opens the door and the father rushes in, looking for his wallet. He finds it, goes through the same kissing routine, looks at the maid and leaves. Everyone begins to get ready to go when the bell rings again. The maid opens the door and lets the father in. This time he is looking for his home and office keys which he finds. He kisses the children and his wife and rushes out. Everyone continues with his preparations but a few minutes later, the maid opens the door again for the father. This time he is looking for his car keys. The mother finds the keys and hands them to him. He apologizes and wants to kiss her, but she pushes him out of the door and this time locks the door and puts the chain on.

Everybody is waiting for the father to come home again but he does not come. They all let out a sigh of relief. When the children are ready to go, the mother cannot find the keys to the car and suddenly, remembers that the father took the keys and the car; he was supposed to go to work with his neighbor. Furiously, she picks up her phone to call him to come back and bring her the car but to her surprise she hears the ringing of a cell phone; the father has forgotten his phone at home!

Following the play, the children went back to the 6 stations until it was time for lunch.

After our good lunch, we gathered in the living room to see another play in pantomime based on my short story that I had written about a family of six entitled Six People with Only One Telephone.

This time the actors were Ori, the father, Shani the mother and Maya, Roni, Alon and Gili the children.

Scene I

A family of six: four teenagers and their parents during the 1980's when the phone in Israel was a luxury and phone calls were expensive; the family possesses one line and it is constantly in use. The arguments among the children occur daily; the father gets complaints from his colleagues that they cannot get in touch with him. And when the phone bill arrives, the father is furious.

Scene II

Everyone is home, watching television. Of course, there is only one television, no cable TV: just one local station or two. The father comes home bearing good news. He brings another phone; the family would be having two lines. The children are happy, and they promise not to talk endlessly on the phone.

Scene III

The children grow up, finish school, go to the army. One by one they move out. The parents remain home alone with their two phones. The phone rings from time to time.

Why pay for two lines. They decide to give one line up.

Scene IV

Now the two parents are left with one line. It is seldom occupied. For a while they are happy. But then people begin walking around with cell phones. It becomes a necessity and the two parents get cellphones. Now there are two people with three lines.

Scene V

Computers are a must in every home. The children and grandchildren come to visit each with their cell phone. Wi-Fi must be installed and so a new router is connected. But there is a special deal that comes with a free phone and line. The parents say they do not need another phone, but this is the deal; take it or leave it. So now two people have four lines but with the e-mails, SMS and WhatsApp, the phones are most of the time silent.

The play left everyone in a good mood and hungry. We had some snacks, played a memory game with our wooden blocks, completed the artistic creations, and still had some time for the big and small games.

The parents came to pick them up at 6 p.m. We had a nice supper together. When the children went home, this time each one remembered to pick up the big bag with all the wonderful gifts, souvenirs, and their own creations.

SUPPLEMENT

The Postcards

One of the reasons that Shalom and I wanted to have this workshop so soon after the last conference was because we wanted to revisit the Italian personalities about whom we had learned in Conference 6. While in Madrid we bought some postcards at the Prado Museum. These postcards were placed at one of the stations together with photos of some famous Italians, their names and a little information on them. The children were supposed to write a postcard and try to mention something about one of the Italian personalities. We decided to share them with you.

Shani (16 ½)

You won't believe who I met. I was walking around innocently along some of the streets in Italy and suddenly I met Leonardo da Vinci! …Leonardo da Vinci! You know Leonardo? You know who he is, right? He was born in 1452, was a man of many traits; a scientist, a mathematician, an engineer, an inventor, a painter, a sculptor, an architect and a musician. Very impressive, no? Leonardo is considered one of the outstanding personalities of the Renaissance and one of the greatest painters of all time.

I can't believe that I actually met him!

Dotan (16)

To my dear cousin,

How are you? I hope that all is well….

I just met Julius Cesar. He told me that he has crowned himself Cesar and has now become the leader of the Roman empire.

Take care

Tamir (15)

To my dear cousin

Last week I visited Italy and you won't believe who I met!

I met Michelangelo himself. He is sculpturing and painting and is involved in architecture, engineering, and poetry. He is one of the greatest painters and one of the most important artists of the Renaissance. We had a long discussion about his Frescos of the Sistine Chapel that is one of the great artistic accomplishments of the Western Civilization. We also spoke about his magnificent statue of David.

Ido (14 ½)

Dear Mother,

Today I reached China via Mongolia. I am surprised to find how different these places are from Italy. In every place I find different customs and cultures. I am keeping a diary and I hope to publish all this in a book.

I miss home but I know that my discoveries will make an important contribution to humanity and knowledge.

Marco Polo

Shira (12 ½)

Christopher Columbus was born in Italy in 1451. He is one of the greatest explorers. He discovered the American continent and opened new naval routes. His discoveries changed the world history. Columbus died in 1506.

Ori (12)

Dante Alighieri lived during the years 1265-1321.

Dante Alighieri was a great poet and wrote the great masterpiece "The Divine Comedy."

Eran (12)

I visited Italy and you wouldn't believe who I met. Galileo Galilei! He is an incredible person. He is a physicist, an astronomer, a mathematician, and an Italian philosopher. His discoveries such as the construction of the first telescope, are astonishing. He improved the heliocentric model of the sun and planets. Galileo is considered the pioneer of modern science and the father of physics. He is also believed to be one of the greatest men of all times.

Maya (11 ½)

During my vacation in Italy, I met Geovanni Lorenzo Bernini. Bernini lived during 1598-1680.

Bernini's sculptures are characterized using high and accurate techniques. He was influenced by the Greek mythology and the stories in the bible. In 1629 he completed the enormous artwork for the San Pietro Basilica in Rome, a project that was began by Michelangelo. Bernini also built the Piazza Navona in Rome and the Fountain of the Four Rivers.

Roni (10 ½)

I visited Italy and I met Raphael Sanzio. Raphael is one of the greatest Italian painters and he was also an architect and considered as one of the pioneers of the Renaissance.

Gili and Alone drew the following beautiful pictures on their postcards.

GILI

ALON

WORKSHOP VII

PERSON OF THE CENTURY

28.11.2015

THE TRIGGER for the workshop this time was the special issue of Time Magazine of December 1999 entitled Person of the Century with the picture of Albert Einstein on the front cover. We decided that it would be a great idea to hold the workshop where the main subject would focus on this issue.

This workshop would involve many lectures throughout the day with relaxing fun activities in between. When we first planned the program, we were worried that it might be too difficult and boring. To our great surprise the children were not only cooperative but also excited and very much involved. So how did we do it? This time most of the credit goes to Shalom.

Decorations

The photo and name of each person of the century by Time Magazine, was scanned, printed, glued onto Bristol paper, and displayed up front to be in full view throughout the day. Besides the photos, stood the Children's World Map and the famous white board.

As usual, we began our workshop with chocolate milk but this time we had my home-baked cheese buns that they all love. There was a little, deliberate delay while I warmed them up and placed them on a very special paper tray together with other "pretend food". What is pretend food? **Post Its** in a variety of sizes and colors in the shape of fruit, vegetables, meat etc.

The special paper tray with the **post it** blocks was unique. I went wild when I first came across this item in one of the shops in Madrid. Imagine a paper tray filled with **post its** of an entire meal; one of meat, one in the shape of a vegetable, one in the shape of a fruit, a slice of toast and so on. I had to remove the meat **post it** to make room for the cheese buns.

As soon as we brought these to the table, every face lit up with excitement. The joy on each face was well worth the many trips to the different locations in Madrid to find 11 sets.

In order to entice the children into a more cooperative mood during the many lectures, we decided that instead of handing out the different "give away" presents all at once or at the end of the day, they would receive a gift before each lecture. You may call this bribery, but we were concerned that most of them were still too young to listen to lectures on "grown up topics". Our worries were unjustified although the little in between gifts helped Alon and Gili to sit through most of the lectures.

Once the table was cleared, the children received their second souvenir, the new special bags: *blue back packs* for the boys and *purple shopping bags* for the girls, both made of light, sturdy and washable material. They put their **post it** treasures inside and put the bags away.

And then we had another surprise for them, t-shirts: for the girls we bought *yellow t-shirts* with "emojis" that are used when sending WhatsApp messages and for the boys we bought *black t-shirts* with the *"evolution of man."* They all changed into the new t-shirts, including Shalom.

I must take a detour and tell you the story behind the t-shirts. Shalom and I were on our way to the biggest Department store in Madrid, Il Corte Ingles, to see what we could pick up for the Workshop. In Madrid, there are a few branches of this well-known store, but the biggest one is located on the Paseo de la Castellana. This huge department store, where I have gotten lost several times and it had taken me a long time to find the right entrance out, is the closest to the Residencia, where Shalom and I stay whenever we go to Madrid. It was still quite a walk, about 4 kilometers. We were almost at the store when at the corner, close to the entrance to one of the metro stations, stood a stand with t-shirts. As soon as we saw them, we both wanted them. We bought 12 and could have taken a taxi back to our room, but Shalom decided to walk back with the purchases. I went on ahead to the Department Store and waited for him in one of the inside bars.

To get back to our workshop, once the participants were seated around the clean table attired in their new t-shirts, Shalom told them that his lectures today are "The Person of the Century in the last millennium (1000 years), as chosen by the special issue of Time Magazine in 1999. He held up the magazine for everyone to see and then continued.

Shalom

"Before I begin my lecture, I would like to hear your opinion on how the candidates should be chosen. Should this important person be a politician, a general, an artist, a scientist or another professionalist?"

This was followed by a very interesting discussion and led the way to a cooperative mood. He told them to save their suggestions for other candidates for later when they would be having a discussion together on this subject. I could tell by the smiles on their faces that this made them feel grown up. Already Shalom was off to a good start.

First Part of Lectures

Shalom

11th **Century** (1000-1099): **William the Conqueror,** king of England, lived from 1027 to 1087. He was a brave soldier and a very clever military leader. He arrived from Normandy (which today is France), in 1066 and conquered England. He initiated bureaucracy that lasted for 800 years.

Subject of Discussion with the participants

Life in England before the arrival of William the Conqueror.

12th Century (1100-1199) **Saladin** who lived from 1138 to 1193 was the first sultan of Egypt and Syria, who ruled Egypt, Syria, Upper Mesopotamia (Middle East and parts of Turkey and Iraq today), the Hejaz (part of Saudi Arabia today), Yemen and North Africa. He was the sultan from 1174 to 1193. He was a Sunni Muslim of Kurdish ethnicity. He won the Muslim military campaign against the Crusader State in the Middle East and conquered Jerusalem. His influence was felt for many centuries.

Subject of Discussion with the participants

How did doctors treat the patients in those days? Did you know that Maimonides, (Rambam), the Jewish great philosopher and religious scholar was Saladin's family doctor in Egypt?

13th Century (1200-1299): **Genghis Khan** the "oceanic ruler" from Mongolia, lived from 1167 to 1227 and reigned from 1206 to 1227. He (followed by his son and grandson) conquered an empire from Asia to Europe. He created the greatest well-organized aggressive army known. His empire connected the civilized China to the rest of the world and lasted to the rule of his grandson Batu, who conquered Russia and Europe and ruled the largest territory empire in history.

Subject of Discussion with participants

Did you know that gun powder was invented by the Chinese in the 9th century and used later by the English to develop guns in the 14th century?

Did you know that Marco Polo, the Italian merchant and writer, traveled to Persia and China along the silk road between 1267 to 1337?

Now it is time for an art project with Safta and we will continue later.

I could see some disappointment on those who were ready to continue but as soon as I distributed the pages of some interesting images that we took out of a paint by number magazine the smiles returned. Shalom had stabled the pages onto Bristol and we made sure that we had enough copies so that a participant could do more than one. This was a big hit with Alon and Gili, especially with the new markers. After an hour of relaxation, laughing and working in a cheerful atmosphere, we cleared the tables and were ready for the second round of talks, but not before having a light snack.

Second part of lectures

Shalom

14th Century (1300-1399): **Giotto** the Italian artist who was the first one to paint real faces and secular paintings, lived from 1267 to 1337. He was the painting pioneer of the Renaissance.

<u>Subject for Discussion with the participants</u>
Was this important enough to choose him as the man of the century?

15th Century: (1400-1499) **Johann Gutenberg** lived from 1395 to 1468. He was a German who invented the printing press.

Subject for Discussion with the participants

The first printed book was the Bible.

The importance of books. How would our world be today without the great invention of printing?

16th Century: (1500-1599): **Queen Elizabeth I** who lived from 1533 to 1603 was queen of England from 1558 to 1603. She made England a global empire. She was the most remarkable woman ruler in history. She gave her name to an age. She was a strong and clever woman who is considered as the first feminist.

Subject for Discussion with the participants

Does she deserve to be the person of this century, considering that during this period we also had Copernicus, Leonardo da Vinci, and Michelangelo?

It was time for a short break again, for the children to stretch their legs and to receive another gift which this time included a pencil case: small, compact, and practical. Then everyone had some water, a quick chat with his neighbor and Shalom continued.

Third Part of Lectures

Shalom

17th Century (1600-1699): **Sir Isaac Newton** was one of the greatest scientists of all time who lived from 1642 to 1727. He discovered the mechanical laws of motion and the force of gravitation.

Since he was one of our heroes from previous meetings, the children agreed unanimously with this choice.

18th **Century** (1700-1799) **Thomas Jefferson** who lived from 1743-1826 was a great American statesman, one of the Founding Fathers, the principal author of the American Constitution and the third President of the United States of America during 1801-1809.

Subject for Discussion with the participants

The discussion this time was devoted to his main belief, "all men are created equal" that he wrote in 1776 in the Declaration of Independence and in the Constitution. Shalom also asked them how this can be compared to the reality of then and today?

19th **Century** (1800-1899): **Thomas Edison** who lived from 1847 to 1931, was a great inventor who invented the "method of invention," as quoted in the Time magazine by Alfred Whitehead. He is considered the father of our high-tech industry.

Subject of Discussion with the participants

The children discussed Edison's statement that "Genius is about 2 percent inspiration and 98 percent perspiration" Shalom promised them that later they will discuss other inventions.

20th **Century** (1900-1999): **Albert Einstein** lived from 1879 to 1955. He was one of our famous scientists in our previous meetings. There was no doubt whatsoever that he was the best choice.

When the discussion was over, the children received pencils to put into their new pencil cases. Then they continued with the painting by number until it was time to eat.

Lunch took a little longer than usual. When everyone finished his meal, we brought out the special wine glasses that the children had painted during Workshop 6 and raised a toast to Shani. She was soon enlisting into the army and it was time for her cousins to wish her success. We all lingered on a little longer just chatting.

Then the participants went into the grandchildren's room while Shalom and I prepared the living room for a mini bazaar which turned out to be a little disappointing this year. Why? We decided to give the children real money instead of the monopoly bills. Each child received 100 shekels for spending. I was sure that they would spend it all. I had especially bought for this occasion a variety of exclusive things. Good bottles of cologne for the boys, nice silver pendants for the girls, scarfs for both the boys and the girls and a variety of items from Madrid: including small interesting games for one, puzzles, small writing boards with their own special markers, games and other small gimmicks. I had spent a lot of money and time; more than in the previous bazaars and was sure that we would have a sellout.

The items were grouped into three sections according to cost:

50 shekels for the cologne and the pendants

20 shekels for the scarfs

15 shekels for all the miscellaneous.

SUMMARY OF THE BAZAAR

All the bottles of cologne were sold.

Only one participant bought a pendant.

Only one bought a scarf.

Some of the small things were sold.

Most of the participants preferred the cash.

Following the bazaar, the children put the things that they had bought and the remaining cash in their bags and Shalom continued. This time it was about inventions and inventors.

Shalom

"Inspired by the previous lectures, where the Time Magazine chose Thomas Edison as the man of the 19th century, I decided to introduce you to a few more inventions and their inventors. But first I want to go back to Thomas Edison. He is considered the greatest American inventor and sometimes even referred to as the father of "high-tech industry". He discovered many devices for electric power generation (the bulb), sound recording and motion pictures.

There were many other exciting inventions by other inventors, but I will mention just a few."

The airplane:

was invented and flown by **the Wright brothers** (Wilbur and Orville). 1903, was the launching of the first flight where the plane was in the air for 12 seconds advancing 37 meters. Shalom asked if the airplane could have been developed before in their opinion. One of the participants raised his hand and said that he remembered from our past conference and workshops that Leonardo da Vinci already considered human flying machines about 500 years previously and he was surprised that it took so long to invent the airplane.

The television:

John Logie Baird was a Scottish engineer who was a pioneer of the television. His first tv picture was developed in 1924 and the first public broadcast of a tv show was from his studio to the London Coliseum Cinema. Baird developed a color TV in 1928 and a stereo TV in 1946.

Basketball:

Was invented in 1891 by the Canadian physical education instructor **James Naismith**. He invented this game so that his students could play indoors with a soccer ball during the winter. The first public game was in the USA in 1892 and in 1936 this game was played at the Olympics in Berlin, Germany where the USA received the gold Medal. Naismith himself attended this Olympic game.

The Battery:

The Italian **Alessandro Volta** invented the first chemical battery in 1800. This battery is a device that converts chemical energy into electrical energy. There are different types of energy: mechanical energy, potential energy, thermal energy, and nuclear energy.

World Wide Web (WWW):
The British scientist **Berner-Lee Tim,** who worked at the European accelerator facility at CERN, Geneva in Switzerland developed the "www" for the sharing of scientific data quickly between physicists and engineers doing research in particle physics around the world.
The children were well informed on this topic and how www changed the world.

Shalom finished this talk by reading out a list of 40 patents, their inventors, and the country where the invention took place.

It was time for a small snack, to move around to stretch their legs and then they were back at the table, this time for origami, jewelry making and games but not before another gift; a special pencil that put a smile on each face. They put their pencils away, each one making sure to put it into his own pencil case and inside the bag.

When they were seated and ready, Shalom, took the famous "white board". He told the children now after having heard his lectures, he wanted them to choose the candidates, who in their opinion, should have been selected for the person of the century. He told them that they should propose a name and he would write it on the board adding that they could choose the same person who had been chosen by the Time Magazine or think of other choices. Then they would have a vote. They could give their votes to as many candidates as they wanted to, which meant that they could raise their hands several times. This was carried out in a very grown up and orderly manner. There was no shouting. Everyone waited patiently for his or her turn.

Here are the children's suggestions and results of the voting:

- David Ben Gurion 2
- Mozart 3
- Nelson Mandela 3
- Genghis Khan 2
- Steve Jobs 2
- Johann Gutenberg 9
- Theodor Herzl 3
- Leonardo da Vinci 3
- Queen Elizabeth I 3
- Sir Isaac Newton 7
- Thomas Jefferson 2
- Thomas Edison 8
- Albert Einstein 9
- Christopher Columbus 5
- The Wright Brothers 2
- Martin Luther King Jr. 3

This session was very exhilarating. The children were very attentive and cooperative and were sorry when it came to an end. To lift their spirits, we gave them the last gift, a pen. As this was the last gift for the day it was not an ordinary pen; it was a feather pen, each one a different color.

We took out the games, the big and the small and we let the children play while Shalom and I set up the table for supper that we were going to have together with their parents.

WORKSHOP VIII

SPAIN AND ITS JEWISH HISTORY

22.10.2016

SHALOM and I have been going to Madrid for one month each year since his first sabbatical there in 1992. We decided that it was about time to do a Workshop on Spain, the Jewish History and the Jewish influence on the country until their expulsion.

On our second sabbatical in Madrid 1997-98, we were fortunate to meet the Israeli Cultural Attaché. His son was having a Bar Mitzva and he invited us to join the celebration at the synagogue where we met the Israeli Consul and his wife, the Israeli representative of ZIM and his wife and another nice couple who had come for a two year stay and remained for many years. We all live in Israel and our friendship has survived all these years.

The Cultural Attaché in Madrid gave us a booklet on all the Jewish cities and villages where the Jews had lived in Spain before their expulsion. Shalom based part of his lecture on this booklet.

What was on the program?

We began the day with breakfast that included different types of serial with fresh fruit, dried fruit, and cookies. On the dining room table, stood the in-between-meal "suppressants": a variety of three color mini peppers, cherry tomatoes, cut up mango, a plate of green and red grapes, some dried fruit, nuts, chickpeas (in Hebrew hummus) and some freshly baked cookies. There was a pitcher of cold water, disposable paper cups, bowls and disposable spoons and paper napkins.

Following breakfast, we distributed the pencil cases which included pens, pencils, and small rulers. The big map of Spain, which had been covered, was now revealed. Besides this map, stood the Children's World Map.

Shalom

The first part of my speech is about the Jewish population of Spain; a place the Jewish people had once called home before their expulsion in 1492. I will point out on the map the places where they had lived.

As far back as the Roman empire, Spanish and Portuguese Jews refer to themselves as Sephardic Jews and to the Iberian

Peninsula as Sepharad. Following are the 8 important cities with a significant Jewish influence before their expulsion:

1. **Caceres,** a city in western Spain's Extremadura region.
2. **Cordoba,** a city in the Southern Spanish region of Andalusia. The most famous religious scholar of Judaism and the most internationally acclaimed philosopher of the middle ages, Moses ben Maimon, commonly known as Maimonides and referred to the acronym Rambam, was born here in 1138. In later years, he was the medical doctor for the Sultan of Egypt,
3. **Girona,** a city in Spain's northeastern Catalonia region. The well-known Jewish religious scholar, philosopher, poet, and medical doctor Moses ben Nahman, commonly known as Nachmanides, and is also referred to by the acronym Ramban, was born here in 1194.
4. **Hervas,** a town north of Caceres.
5. **Ribadavia,** a town in the northwestern part of Spain in the region of Galicia.
6. **Segovia,** a city northwest of Madrid in the central Spain Castile and Leon region. (It is said that this majestic site, inspired Walt Disney in the creation of the castle in some of his films).
7. **Toledo,** a city of the Castilla la Mancha in central Spain where the famous painter El Greco lived. Toledo is known as "the city of three cultures",

because of the influence of the Christians, Muslims, and Jews.

8. **Tudela,** a city in northern Spain in the region of Navarre. The famous Jewish traveler in the 13th century Benjamin of Tudela was from this city.

The children needed a break to absorb the important information. We had the perfect thing for them: some fresh snacks while watching a very funny scene from one of Danny Kay's movies.

When they returned to the table again, Shalom had added another, smaller map of Spain. He used pegs that he placed on the eight cities where the Jews had lived before their expulsion in 1492: These pegs remained all day so that the children could walk up to the map and see the places at close range.

Shalom continued:

"Some people claim that the Jews had lived in Spain already during the **biblical times**, however more realistic evidence suggests that the Jews arrived in Spain during the Roman Empire era. For about 1500 years, the Jews lived in Spain until they were expelled in 1492. Before that time, there were good and bad times for the Jews in Spain."

Throughout many centuries, before their expulsion, the Jews in Spain were the largest and most prosperous Jewish community in the world. The Spanish Jews were the leaders of the World Jewry in the philosophical studies as well as in literature, including Hebrew poetry for the first time since the period of the Bible (1500 BC to about 500 BC). In 1492, about 300,000 Jews were converted by decree to Catholicism and about 50,000, those who did not want to convert, were expelled from Spain. Some of the converted Jews continued with the laws of Judaism in hiding and when caught were executed.

There were many great "Spanish Jews" or Sephardi Jews as they are referred to by their descendants. Today I will talk only about four of them, who I think deserve special mention.

Samuel ibn Naghrillah known as Samuel HaNagid from Andalusia lived from 993 until 1056. He was a scholar of the Talmud, a merchant, a soldier and a general.

Subject for discussion with the participants

What was it like being a general in those days?

Solomon ibn Gabirol was an 11th century great poet and philosopher from Andalusia.

He is well known for his statement that everything, including soul and intellect, is made of "matter and form".

Subject for discussion with the participants

What do you think of the above statement?

Judah Halevi was a philosopher, a great poet, and a physician. Born in Toledo (or Tudela) in 1075 and died shortly after arriving to Jerusalem in 1141. The Crusaders ruled Jerusalem during that time. Yehuda Halevi was considered by some people as the greatest Jewish poet of all times. He wrote Hebrew poetry. I chose one of his poems today, which is usually studied in High School in Israel: "Zion, will you not ask…"

Subject for discussion with the participants

Some of them volunteered to read a few lines from the poem because they had learned it in school and were still familiar with it. Then we discussed the poem.

Shalom continued: Judah Halevi also wrote the book The Kuzari, describing a religious-philosophical discussion between a Rabi and the king of Kuzar. Let me show you on the map where Kuzar is located and if such a kingdom existed. Yes, the Khazars did exist; they were a semi-nomadic tribe that ruled the southern part of Russia between the Caspian Sea and the Black Sea for 4 centuries (from the 7th to the 11th).

Moses ben Maimon, was born in Cordoba in 1138 and died in Egypt in 1204. Known as the Maimonides, (his acronym RAMBAM in Hebrew) was the most famous religious scholar in Jewish religion, internationally well-known and a much-liked philosopher of the middle ages. Later in his life he was the medical doctor of Sultan Salah a Din and his family of Egypt as I have mentioned to you before.

Subject for discussion with the participants

The children were familiar with this name not only from our past workshops but also from school. Shalom asked them to discuss how influential and dominant he was in the Jewish religion, during his time and until today.

Then, we let the children get up and stretch their legs, have some water, a little snack, a small chat with a fellow participant and back to the table for the next project.

While in Madrid I came across an interesting magazine in Spanish. It was all about thinking and activities, good diets etc. It was entitled An Active Mind that contained a section with interesting activities. This is what we prepared for the next activity.

A Pleasant Hour of Thinking

The participants were divided into 4 groups according to the different ages. Each group had a different set of questions. Following are the groups:

- **Shani and Dotan**
- **Tamir, Ido and Shira**
- **Ori, Eran, Maya and Roni**
- **Alon and Gili**

Following are the four common assignments given to all the groups:

Write a full length, logical sentence, making it as long as you can, where all the words begin with the same letter.

Make up a list describing objects in nature that are green.

Write with your left hand the sentence "I love my mother and my father." Eran who is left-handed was told to write the sentence with his right hand.

Invent a name for a new Perfume or for a new puppy.

The first three groups received the following common question: in writing all numbers from 200 to 299, how many times does the digit 2 appear (if you want to try it, the answer is 120).

We also prepared some different level questions for the four groups. One interesting question was to identify different European cities where some famous monuments are displayed.

And for the ones who wanted a challenge, we included some IQ test questions.

Of course, the hour that we had allotted for this activity stretched to an hour and a half, but the children were having so much fun that we did not have the heart to stop.

Following this session, they saw a short documentary about nature and then we were all set for our next activity, art. It gave them a chance to relax and to do something together not in a competitive way.

This time, I had picked up a paint by number booklet of famous paintings that were familiar to them from our past meetings. Shalom removed the pages and stapled some of them onto Bristol paper. We numbered them on the back, and everyone received the page according to the lottery. We made sure to make many extras so that if someone was unsatisfied, he could choose another page.

Time flies when you are having fun and I had to cut into this activity because it was already 13:30 and we had to have lunch. The children went to wash their hands and wipe them on their new towels.

Lunch this time consisted of a vegetable soup, honey baked chicken, smashed potatoes in the oven, pasta with fresh tomato sauce, a vegetable salad that included avocado and mango, sweet corn, and sweet baby carrots.

For dessert we had some jelly with fresh fruit.

Following lunch, we went into the living room to see two films:

An animated short film of 4 minutes entitled The Present by Jacob Frey. When I received a copy of it in my mail, it had the subtitle "Whoever sent in the film was offered a job by Disney." It was a beautiful and touching film.

The other one was Charlie Chaplin which is always a big hit and gets everyone laughing.

To continue our relaxing mood, Shalom and I recalled some of our experiences from the many visits to Madrid; places that we visited, invitations to Spanish people's homes, my adventures at the Spanish courses, our two weeks in Salamanca to study Spanish and my cooking class in Madrid.

The children wanted to hear more stories, but we had to continue with our schedule; to finish off their art project. When everyone was done, we had a snack and then went into the living room to see two more short films. The films were: Charlie Chaplin and A hundred years of fashion.

When they returned to the tables again, Shalom was ready with another lecture: "interesting quotes by two famous Spaniards and several by Maimonides (Rambam)":

Pablo Picasso lived between 1881 and 1973. One of the most famous Spanish painters. *"Everything that can be imagined is real"* ; (in Spanish:" Todo lo que puede ser imaginado es real")

Miguel de Cervantes lived between 1547 and 1616, the famous author of the book Don Quixote that was first published in two parts in 1605 and 1615; *"When one door closes, another one opens"* (In Spanish: "Donde una puerta se cierra, otra se obre")

Maimonides (Rambam) lived during 1138-1204. The following quotes are freely translated from Hebrew:

Every person has his own personality. Every person has many thoughts and opinions.

The middle route is the best route, called by Rambam the "golden route".

The least said the better. Therefore, do not hurry to answer a question and do not speak too much.

A person should only eat when he is hungry.

Every person who does not exercise all his life will suffer pains and be weak.

Truth and justice are the jewels of our soul.

Subjects for discussions with the participants:

What do you think of the above quotes?

Following an interesting discussion we had a little snack and then to the living room to see two more short films: *An interesting twist in Britain has talent; the history of the world in 2 minutes.*

And then it was time for our **Bazaar**. This time we used monopoly money. It was a smashing hit and we sold everything.

We were curious what the children thought about this workshop since it involved so many lectures. We had done such a discussion only once before, in Workshop 5, Science and Art, in 2013, three years ago.

We gathered around the table and following are what the children said in Hebrew and our translation to English from the tape-recorded discussion:

Ido, age 16

I enjoyed the workshop very much. I have always enjoyed these get-togethers. I think now that we are older, the lectures were a great part of the workshop. I personally enjoyed them very much.

Alon, age 9

I enjoyed the workshop very much. I also enjoyed the lectures, but I especially enjoyed the short films and all the other activities.

Shani, age 18

I enjoyed this workshop very much. The combination of the short films in between the lectures made it possible for me to concentrate better on the lectures. As always, I also enjoyed the artwork and the bazaar. To me all the conferences and Workshops that we had, have always been very enjoyable.

Eran, age 14

I really enjoyed the workshop and especially the subject this year on Spain. I liked the lectures and found them very interesting.

Tamir, age 17

I enjoyed the workshop very much as I always do. I agree with Shani that the combination of short films and lectures was a great idea especially that the short films were on so many diverse topics. The food was great, the company excellent. With such a fantastic cook, what else could one want; nothing was missing.

Roni, age 13

I had a great time. The food was good, I enjoyed the bazaar and the lectures and especially the participation of the participants.

Gili, age 7

I had a great time. I enjoyed everything.

Maya, age 14

I had a great time. I agree with Shani. The idea of having the lectures with breaks with a variety of films made everything very enjoyable. I had a great time.

Shira, age 15

I really enjoyed this workshop. I had a great time. I liked the short films and, I found the lectures interesting,

Ori, age 14

I really enjoyed this workshop. I liked the lectures very much and everything else and hope that we will have more of these types of workshops and conferences.

Dotan, age 18

I really enjoyed Saba's lectures. It is not the first time that I have heard him lecturing and I always go away with a good taste for more. I also enjoyed the films and tried to be "creative" with the paint by number picture. And I also enjoyed Eran's jokes.

At the end of this discussion, Shalom summarized in a humoristic manner, "I will try to review what you have all said, namely, that we should send in a proposal to the Ministry of Education and suggest that the children should have lectures in school together with funny short films like Charlie Chaplin; ten minutes a lecture and ten minutes a funny film; then the children will be very happy to go to school."

I said I am glad that they all enjoyed my cooking and preparations.

After a round of applause, the children went into the living room to see Shani's musical presentation that she had prepared a couple of years ago using photos from the first 4 conferences and Workshop 1.

While the children watched, I went to the kitchen to set up the tables for supper together with the parents.

This time supper included meatballs, beef cooked in the

oven with wine, rice with a sauce made from fresh tomatoes, smashed potatoes, a vegetable salad, sweet carrots and left-over corn from lunch, a special cabbage salad and baked vegetables in the oven. Dessert consisted of a fresh fruit salad and freshly baked chocolate cookies with puffed rice and cranberries.

WORKSHOP IX

FUN WITH COUSINS FROM TORONTO IN ENGLISH

1.1.2017

THIS WORKSHOP WAS ESPECIALLY ORGANIZED for the grandchildren to have a special fun day together with their cousins from Toronto on their second visit to Israel during the Hanukkah vacation. It was a great visit. It gave us the opportunity to light the Hanukkah candles together with the children and grandchildren, every evening in a different home. This year the eighth candle was on Saturday the 31st of December. As we were still in the Hanukkah mood, Shalom decided that one of his lectures would be dedicated to this Jewish Holiday.

The program was from 10 in the morning until 6:30 in the evening, when the parents would join us for supper. In between the two meals, we had cut up vegetables, fruit and popcorn during the films.

So, what did we have on the program for this day? At Workshop 8, the children had such a good time with the combination of serious lectures and short films, we decided to repeat this type of schedule. The language used on this day was mostly English because the children were all older and almost all of them had a good knowledge of English. This made it much easier than at our last Workshop with our Canadian relatives five years ago.

Today, we had a late breakfast that included orange juice and a variety of serials and chocolate milk, soy milk or coffee. After everyone finished eating and the tables were cleared, each one received his individual towel that he or she hung up in the two washrooms: one for the girls and one for the boys. Then they also received small writing pads and pens. Before we began, I collected all their smartphones and placed them in a basket, a procedure we followed in our conferences and workshops as the children got older.

Before this workshop, I had picked up a magazine in the bookshop with all the flags of the world. There were 192 different flags. We cut these out and dispersed them on the table.

The Children's World Map stood in waiting for Shalom to point out the different locations around the globe.

FLAGS OF THE WORLD

Shalom

Flags are the symbols of countries. In the Bible, the book of Numbers, chapter 2,2 we read "The Israelites are camping …. each one sitting under the banners of his own tribe". As far back as over 3,000 years ago, the symbol of identification was by a banner.

The participants were then divided into 5 groups and shared the 192 flags that we had cut out of the booklet. Shalom asked the participants to find unusual looking flags such as Nepal (two triangles), Andorra, (2 cows) and so on. Shalom together with the children, found all the countries and the continent of each of the 192 flags. They found 49 flags from Europe, 53 from Africa, 43 from Asia, 33 from the Americas and 14 from Australia and Oceania.

Shalom

Now we shall concentrate on the USA and Canada. Since the USA declaration of independence, there have been 28 changes to the famous USA Stars and Stripes Flag. For example, the second USA flag from 1777 to 1795 had 13 stars. Canada had several flags until the current one which was introduced in 1965. Of course, our Canadian participants know this.

When Israel became an independent state in 1948, with the

population of 800,000, the flag was founded and has never changed.

Following the interesting lecture (according to our audience) we had a 15-minute break to see 2 short films with popcorn served in paper cups with endless refills.

When they returned to the tables, I asked them to take their writing pads and write about an imaginary dream involving the few words that I wrote on the white board. I borrowed this idea from my Italian teacher. She gave us this exercise in Italian, and it was such a success, that I decided to do this exercise with the participants, and it was successful here too. The children put on their thinking caps and a few nice imaginary tales were told. Jesse, the youngest of the 3 Canadians cousins, received the loudest applause when he read his piece.

We returned to the living room to see two more short films, this time without popcorn.

When they returned to the table, they were surprised to see a non-symmetrical small pitcher filled with raw beans. They were supposed to guess how many beans were in the pitcher. To make the guessing even harder, we stuffed quite a few white paper towels on the bottom to take up some of the space (I also did not have enough beans). The children had to guess how many beans were inside. Some of the older ones tried to use mathematics but in this case it was useless. In total there were 1025 beans; it was Jesse who came the closest. Following are the numbers:

- Jesse 828
- Ori 780
- Eran 717
- Roni 635
- Dotan 580
- Samantha 567
- Shira 430
- Shani 425
- Alon 370
- Tamir 343
- Ido 335
- Maya 320
- Aaron 274
- Gili 2050

For relaxation, we gave each child a paint by number reproduction of a famous monument or attraction. They were very pleased with this assignment and so absorbed in their work that when I told them that we are going into the living room to see two more short films, some begged for a little more time. So, I allowed them an additional 10 minutes and told them that whoever did not finish his masterpiece would do it later.

Following the short films, while I was getting the food ready, Shalom did an exciting exercise with them. I received by email a magnificent image that contained many smaller diverse images inside. We loaded the image on the screen of our television and the children had to find the different little images or faces hidden in the big one. They were very pleased with this exercise and had to be lured back to the table for lunch.

We had a nice lunch hour. They golfed down the food. They were hungry and maybe they enjoyed the food.

Following lunch, we had another short film break, this time without popcorn.

Then we had our special art project. Each participant received a white t-shirt and had to design his own creation with the special coloring markers used on cloth. As soon as the masterpiece was completed, it was turned upside down and given to Shalom to steam press for long lasting color preservation. Then, each one put on his t-shirt and had his photo taken. By the smiles on their faces, they were all pleased with their designs.

Before Shalom's next lecture we returned to the living room to see a short documentary entitled "How the People had Lived One Century ago."

Shalom

One hundred years ago, the following were still not invented: the mobile telephone, the electronic computer, nor the television.

Some statistics in the USA and Canada in the year 1916, a 100 years ago:

The average life expectancy for men was 47 years.

Only 14% of homes had a bathtub.

Only 8% of homes had a telephone, which meant that out of every100 homes, 92 did not have one.

Only 6% of all Americans had graduated from high school.

The maximum speed limit of cars in most cities was 10 miles per hour (16 kilometers per hour) **Fuel** for cars was sold in drug stores only.

95% of all births were at home.

95% of all Doctors had no College Education.

Canada passed a law that prohibited poor people from entering the country for any reason.

The USA flag had 45 stars.

The population of Las Vegas, Nevada was only 35.

The tallest building in the world was the Eifel Tower in Paris, France.

Now I want to show you some images from that **period:** a hair dryer in 1920 in a beauty salon; a telephone engineer working in London in 1927; changing the street lamps in 1910; the cars and bicycles then; and the photo of a woman who was considered beautiful during that period.

Can you imagine what it will be like in 100 years from today?

The children put on their thinking caps and came up with some great thoughts. Too bad that we did not tape this session.

As you know by now, every lecture is followed by a short film, this time with popcorn again.

Then we returned to the table for Shalom's next lecture entitled "The Emblem of the State of Israel":

Shalom

The Emblem of the state of Israel was adopted on the 10th of February 1949 following a design competition in 1948.

The emblem is depicted with a menorah with a seven-branched candelabrum with an olive branch on each side with the inscription ISRAEL in Hebrew. As is well known, the olive branch also symbolizes Peace.

We come across parts of this emblem in the bible, the book of exodus where there is a description of the seven lamps made of gold and used in the portable sanctuary built by Moses in the desert. About 300 years later, this menorah was included in the Temple in Jerusalem built by King Solomon, the son of King David. About 500 years later, during the establishment of the Second Temple, in the book of Zechariah, chapter 4, there is the description, by this prophet, of a menorah with two olive trees, one on each side.

The menorah, being carried on the backs of the Jews, taken from the temple in Jerusalem, is also portrayed on the Arch of Titus in Rome. These Jews were captured by the Roman soldiers after the Jewish revolt and the destruction of the Second Temple in 70 AD.

Shalom ended this lecture by showing the children pictures of the different Menorahs found in old excavations and synagogues, as well as the different designs that were proposed in the competition in 1948.

After his lecture, we were back to see another short film which was followed yet by another lecture: "Surprising Geographical Facts."

Shalom

Did you know that geography was originally a Greek word meaning "earth description"? Today it is considered a science devoted to land, its phenomena, and its inhabitants. I will show you some maps with my lectures.

The oldest world map is from the 9th century BC (almost 3000 years ago) designed by the ancient Babylonian civilization. The Greeks were the first to explore Geography, beginning about the year 600 BC.

Today we shall discuss some surprising facts in Geography. I am sure you are familiar with some of them:

1. Canada has more lakes than the rest of the world combined. I see that our Canadian participants are smiling because they know this already. But did you know that the meaning of the word Canada means "Big Village" as was originally given by the Canadian Indians in their language? They are smiling again so I presume that they already knew this as well.

2. Damascus, Syria was founded more than 4500 years ago and is the oldest continuously inhabited city that exists today.

3. The first city in the world to reach a population of one million was Rome, Italy during the big Roman empire.
The city of New York has more:
(a) Jews than in Tel Aviv, Israel
(b) Irish than in Dublin, Ireland
(c) Italians than in Rome, Italy

4. Istanbul, Turkey is the only city in the world located on two continents, Europe and Asia.

5. Antarctica is the only continent on our planet that does not belong to any country in the world; Although 90% of the ice in the world is in Antarctica, it is a desert because it almost never rains.

It was time for a break; like a recess in school; a little snack, a trip to the washroom, an exchange of some words with another participant and they were back to see another short film before Shalom's final lecture for the day "Hanukkah."

Shalom

As you know, we have just finished celebrating Hanukkah and I am sure that you enjoyed lighting the Hanukkah candles, as much as we all did, every evening somewhere else. They were special to all of us.

Whoever has learned or read about Hanukkah, knows about the heroism of the Maccabees and the rededication of the Second Temple in Jerusalem. In Israel there is a very popular song about the Maccabees that the children learn in kindergarten. This song is also sung in almost every home during Hanukkah.

Today I would like to present a historical perspective of this happy holiday.

The first Jewish independent state with Jerusalem its

capital and its first Temple lasted about 4 centuries, from 1000 BC to 600 BC.

Hanukkah is the celebration of the **Second Jewish Independent State**. This independence lasted 77 years, from 140BC to 63BC. BC refers to the time before the birth of Christ.

It took the Jewish people another 2000 years to obtain the Jewish **Third Independent State** in 1948, following the War of Independence.

The perspective that I want to present to you now is who ruled Israel during more than 3000 years.

Moses took the Jews out of slavery in Egypt about 1300 BC.

Joshua settled them around 1250 BC in Canaan lands, with the 12 Jewish tribes who called themselves Israel.

King David, 1000BC conquered Jerusalem and made it the capital and center of Israel. King Salomon, son of David, built the first Temple in Jerusalem.

After Salomon's death the country was divided into 2 states, Judea with 2 tribes and its Capital Jerusalem, and Israel that contained 10 tribes (out of the 12). Israel was destroyed in 722BC.

The Babylonians, who also destroyed the first temple, ruled Judea for one century.

The Persians ruled the following 2 centuries until 300 BC. During this rule, the second temple in Jerusalem was built.

The Greek Empire ruled Jerusalem and Judea until the Maccabean revolt that lasted more than 20 years. We celebrate Hanukkah to honor this independence which lasted for 77 years, from 140BC to 63BC.

The Roman Empire occupied Judea. After 130 years of Roman rule and after a Jewish new revolt, the Second Temple was destroyed in the year 70 AD.

Throughout 19 centuries, Israel was ruled by Romans, Byzantines, the Arabs, the Crusaders, the Mamelukes, the Ottoman Empire and the British. In 1948, following the war of independence, Israel became an independent state for the third time.

Today, almost every Jewish household in Israel and abroad celebrates the eight days of Hanukkah by lighting the Hanukkah candles for the eight days. We enjoy eating the traditional potato pancakes (levivot) and special doughnuts (sufganiot) and sing the Hanukkah songs. It has also become customary to give the children Hanukkah money. So now I have the pleasure to give each one of you "Dmei Hanukka" (as known in Hebrew for Hanukkah money); for our Canadian participants we also bought some special dreidels.

The children took their note pads, pens, towels, t-shirts, and other small souvenirs of the day and each one put all his treasures in his own bag.

The parents arrived at 6:30. Some helped to set up the tables for supper. The children were excited showing off their accomplishments of the day. We had a cheerful supper which was a nice finale to a great day.

WORKSHOP X

WE DID IT OUR WAY

November 9, 2019

A few months previously

SHALOM and I are in Madrid again. Before we went abroad, we had many discussions with our grandchildren regarding another workshop. The requests came from all of them, the younger and the older ones as well. Today, Shani has finished the army service and is now working part time and studying part time. Dotan has finished his first degree in physics and is now in the army. Tamir and Ido are in the army too. Shira has graduated from school, worked part time, is now on a trip to New York with a friend for two weeks and is enlisting in the army in the Spring. Ori and Eran will be graduating at the end of the year;

Maya and Roni are in High School and will be graduating in two years. Alon is in the first year of Junior High and little Gili is in grade 5. How could we say no to another workshop! All we had to do was to find a suitable day for everyone, a task more difficult than in the past. Even more difficult was to plan an interesting program for 12 participants ages 10 to 21. This was certainly a challenge.

While Shalom was at work at the Institute in Madrid, I spent many hours thinking. Different ideas came and went but nothing seemed good enough to make this day enjoyable and still maintain our standards?

I went on exploration tours to find suitable items to buy. Shalom and I spent hours discussing different ideas; we went out to different coffee shops in Madrid, hoping that the calming atmosphere would enable us to think better. Many ideas were considered and rejected.

When Shalom suggested to visit some of the museums, I took him shopping instead. He did not complain because he too was anxious to come up with a good program.

As the days slipped by, I became concerned. We spent more time in bookstores, department stores and museum shops. Then one day we found tote bags for the boys and nice handbags for the girls; it was a good start. We also found good quality pencils and pens, rulers imprinted with well-known sayings and special artistic folders at the museum stores. We bought school supplies at a store catering to schools and universities. Then I found some small gimmicks that I thought were special and that the children would enjoy. Our feet made a lot of mileage but at least we did not return to Israel empty handed.

The first thing on the agenda was coordinating a suitable date. The holidays had come and gone; if one participant was free, another one was busy with a scout trip, a best friends' birthday party; and our soldiers could not always be available. But miraculously, we managed to find one magic Saturday that was suitable for everyone, November 9th.

Before I got busy with the workshop, I had to start shopping and cooking for the Yom Kippur Holiday. Shalom and I have a tradition that our two children and grandchildren who live in Rehovot come to have the two meals with us (before the fast and after the fast). They come with their vehicles; park them in our parking area; walk home after the meal. The next day, following the fast, they walk to our house or take the other car, partake of the meal and drive back home.

Following the holiday, Shalom and I dedicated all our spare time for planning the program. Although we had come up with several ideas in Madrid, we still had a lot of work to do. We spent hours revising the program.

As the time was nearing to the deadline, we spent endless discussions and incorporated many changes. Finally, when we decided that we had the last version, I typed up the program. But when we reviewed it again, we had to introduce a few more changes. At first Shalom did the changes by hand but when this became too disorderly, he retyped the program and printed the new version.

Once the program was final, we went shopping for: 12 hand towels, 12 t-shirts, 12 disks on key, 12 notebooks, etc. On Thursday, before the Workshop I went to the French Patisserie in Rehovot to prepay in advance for the Croissants so that children could have them with their chocolate milk or coffee Saturday morning. On Friday, the lineup is so long that it stretches from inside the store, along the sidewalk as far as the road. But if you order the day before, you can avoid the queue and pick up your purchase quickly.

As usual Shalom took off a few days from work to finish our preparations. I was busy cooking the meals for the participants and for the supper with their parents. He was busy washing, labeling and running out to get things that we had forgotten to buy. Shani came three times during the few weeks before, a couple of hours each time, to prepare some of the special surprises for all the participants; all this, later.

The Day of the Workshop

As you already know by now, I become anxious before the start of these get togethers, but this time I was even more concerned. I do not know why; maybe because they had all grown up and become more sophisticated. Or maybe it is because this is the way I am and can't change.

This time the menu for the day was posted at the entrance:

Breakfast

Chocolate milk or any other hot or cold drink

Chocolate Butter Croissants

Slices of Hallah with white cheese, chocolate spread or peanut butter

Lunch

Chicken Soup

Honey Coated Chicken

Turkey Roast

Rice, Sweet Corn, and Smashed Potatoes

A green salad

Coleslaw

Jelly

Non-dairy ice cream cubes

Snacks after breakfast until lunch

Snacks after lunch until supper

Supper with the parents

·   ·   ·

Shalom and I had set up the tables and prepared the last-minute arrangements. The croissants were removed from the freezer and set to thaw. We had a few minutes of relaxation before battling the hard day ahead.

They arrived promptly at 10 a.m. This time they all came by themselves because each family has at least one participant with a driver's license.

It was nice to see them so excited! They were happy to be together; as noisy as when they were small; they were still children after all. Immediately my confidence returned.

Before they sat down for the morning bite, we handed out the new t-shirts that we had bought, olive green for the girls and black for the boys. They were asked to put them on while the tags were still on because I was not sure about the sizes. Amazingly, they all fit perfectly.

Soon all the price tags were removed, and everyone put on the new t-shirt. We made some group pictures and one of each participant alone on the lazy boy, like we have done for almost all the workshops and conferences. Following the picture taking, each one received their own new hand towels which they immediately went to hang up. Then they received the water bottles; each with his or her name; the same bottle that they have been using since Conference 2. (The ones from Conference 1 had been taken home). Amit received a new bottle that included an inside supplement for ice or fruit, to make the water tastier. If one of the participants was a little envious of the new practical bottle, he or she did not show it. Each one filled his bottle with cold water and took his place at one of the tables.

When everyone was seated and it was quiet I continued.

Yaffa

Today, 12 years have passed since we convened our first conference. We still feel as excited as in 2007.

Before Saba says a few words, I want to thank Shani who has prepared a new, exciting musical presentation that includes Conferences 5 and 6 and Workshops 2 to 9. I am sure that you remember the marvelous job that she did on the presentation of the first 4 conferences and Workshop 1 a few years ago. For those who have forgotten or not seen it, you will have a chance to see it later. I know that you are going to enjoy this new one too. She also spent many hours before this meeting preparing more surprises that you will get to see later. Let's have a round of applause for Shani! (Everyone applauded heartily.)

Also, we have a "guest" today. Someone you all know so well. Amit we are honored that you could join us today. A round of applause for Amit!! (Again, all the children applauded happily.)

Shalom

I am sure that you will all enjoy this day. By now you know that Safta comes up with good ideas.

Now, as you know, the title of this workshop is "We Did It Our Way" and we did. I think this is a very appropriate title because we took many different topics, ideas big and small, difficult and versatile and we did it our way to make it suitable for you during the different conferences and workshops.

Today we shall revisit our 6 conferences and the 9 workshops. We will try to recall the past with a perspective to the future. We shall see some short films in accordance with these thoughts and take a quick glimpse into the energy problem of the past, the present and the prospects for the future.

Our first conference was held in 2007. Many things have changed since then and keep on changing all the time. I would like to quote two individuals whom I greatly admire: the Israeli first prime minister, David Ben Gurion, who said: "We have to know and appreciate the past, but we have to live for the future." And another famous quote by Albert Einstein: "imagination is more important than knowledge."

Keeping these two quotes in mind, always remember that knowledge of our past is imperative, but imagination is more important for our future success.

The time is short, and we have a lot to do, so let us get started. We hope you enjoy this workshop!

We went into the living room to watch the musical presentation of the first 4 conferences and the very first workshop that Shani had prepared a few years ago. The participants were excited to see how much they had grown. This presentation was followed by a short film showing life in the United States years ago, before the era of television, computers, mobile phones and many other items that today are taken for granted. Then the second musical presentation by Shani that she had prepared especially for this Workshop was shown; this time it included Conferences 5 and 6 and Workshops 2 to 9. The children were excited to see themselves changing and how the progress of learning had advanced throughout the conferences and workshops. This was followed by a very short film about a new Israeli technological development, called the bracelet that eventually may replace smartphones and tablets. To conclude this entertaining session, we screened three films; two very short humorous and one about magic.

A little Bit of Learning

We then watched a very short, serious film from the TV about the Big Bang Theory and what followed. This film was four minutes long, quick and fascinating and a good preparation for Shalom's talk on this serious topic.

Shalom

You have seen this well-made short film about the **Big Bang Theory** and the creation of galaxies, our sun, and our planet Earth. Now for some scientific numbers related to these events:

To make sure that this will be clear to all the participants, a small reminder that 1000 times 1000 is a million; one thousand million is referred to in some countries (USA) as one billion and by others (Israel) a milliard.

According to the **Big Bang Theory** the Universe was

created about **13,700 million** years ago. All the energy of our Universe, a short time after its creation, was in the beginning in a plasma state of matter.

Our galaxy was created about 13,300 million years ago, **400 million** years following the **Big Bang Explosion.**

It took another **9,000 million** years for our **Sun** to be created. Our sun is one out of (about) 200 billion stars that make up our **Galaxy**, known as the **Milky Way,** where many of its stars are seen at night. The **Sun** and our **Galaxy**, as well as other galaxies are mostly in a plasma state of matter.

About **4,500 million** years ago our planet **Earth** was created. Today, all the states of matter on our planet are solid, liquid and gas. The plasma state of matter can be achieved in the laboratory or occasionally occurs by nature during a thunderstorm.

The big dinosaurs disappeared **66 million** years ago; the first primitive human being (someone like Lucy) appeared about 5 million years ago. The modern human being (Homo sapiens) appeared about **300,000** years ago, while civilization began only **10,000** years ago. For reference, the Jewish history dates back **4500** years.

Now let's go back to the three states of matter, a subject that we already learn in school: the solid, liquid and gas. But there is also a fourth state known as plasma. When you heat up a solid such as a cube of ice, it turns into a liquid (water). If the liquid is heated some more, it turns into a gas (steam). By further heating of the gas, you obtain a different kind of gas the **plasma.** Following are some rhyming verses written by Safta

Yaffa in English in our book The Fourth State of Matter, An Introduction to the Physics of Plasma, Yaffa and Shalom Eliezer, Adam Hilger, 1989 and the Second Edition by the Institute of Physics Publishing, Bristol and Philadelphia 2001. I will translate the lines into Hebrew for those who have difficulty understanding.

The meaning of plasma in medicine is quite ordinary,
A simple explanation can be found in any dictionary.
It's the watery fluid of organic compounds and
mixtures,
In which the cells of the blood are suspended as
permanent fixtures.
Plasma in science is not at all the same,
Although mistakenly it acquired the exact name.
In blood plasma is a liquid, similar to water,
In science plasma is gas and the fourth state of matter.

Iron at room temperature is a solid. If you take a piece of iron and you heat it up to a little more than 1500 degrees Celsius (C) then it becomes a liquid just like ice turns to water at 0 degrees C. If you heat the liquid iron up further, close to 3000 degrees C, then it will become a gas, just like liquid water becomes steam at 100 C. The solid, liquid and gas are 3 states of matter; the different states of matter are determined by their different domains of temperatures. Besides the temperature, the pressure also plays an important role in arriving at the different phases. Pressure in physics is like taking something (gas for example) and squeezing it. The more you squeeze, the higher the pressure. In physics, pressure is known as the force acting on a body divided by the area that the force is acting on.

As you already know, all matter is made up of atoms. Let us use for example iron; it can be in the state of solid or liquid or gas. In all these stages the iron phases are composed of atoms (denoted by Fe in the Mendeleyev Table of elements). Water is made up of molecules, each containing two hydrogen atoms and one oxygen. All the solids, liquids or gas are composed of atoms.

When heating the gas further, its atoms split and lose their electrons, (one or more), depending on the temperature. When this occurs, the gas changes to the fourth state of matter, the plasma. This plasma is composed of freely moving electrons and freely moving ions (those left over from the atoms that have lost some or all their electrons). Thus, the fourth state of matter is a mixture of electrons and ions in motion. The motion depends on temperature and pressure and can be quite complicated, like the waves and turbulences in the oceans.

Most of our Universe is in this fourth state of matter, plasma, just like our Sun. The energy of our universe comes from the nuclear reactions inside the very hot and dense plasmas, as in the center of our Sun. I will discuss this with you in my next lecture when I shall talk about "The Good, the Bad and the Ugly".

Thank you for listening so quietly. I hope it is a sign that you enjoyed this lecture. Now Safta will read her rhyming verse on the Four States of Matter in English and in Hebrew.

Shalom's interesting lecture put the participants in a scientific mood so that they were ready to listen to my rhyming verses about the Four States of Matter in English, taken from Shalom's and mine book on The Fourth State of Matter. I translated these verses into Hebrew myself, a translation that took me many hours, but I was determined to do it on my own.

The Four States of Matter

In the beginning there was nothing at all,
Except for the Universe compressed in a ball.
Then followed the "Big Bang" episode,
Causing the ball to violently explode.
Creating entirely a hot plasma lather,
Which was actually the first state of matter.

After the explosion, the matter cooled down,
Turning the fragments into stars, just like our Sun.
During the expansion of this gigantic heat storm,
Matter cooled down to the gas form.
The cooling continued to liquid and solid formation,
To form the different matter configuration.

In the beginning, with the coming of civilization,
Prehistoric man's first inauguration
Was to the earth and the rocks; the rain and the water.

These solids and liquids became the first and second
states of matter.
The gas was realized later and became the third
phase,
And last came the plasma to interchange from first to
fourth place.

The children were listening quietly while filling up with cut up vegetables. I did not worry because I had prepared a big amount of these healthy snacks.

Before taking our "promenade" through our six conferences, the children received pencils, pens, notebooks and a stack of *post its*.

Yaffa

I will try to keep my talk brief and to recapture a few highlights about each conference.

Conference Number One in 2007 was originally meant to be a pajama party and did not include a program. We named it "Getting Together" and we did not concentrate on any special topic. We had some games; we introduced our white board; did some amazing origami, and some art. We provided the mattresses, pillows and blankets; we were left with a lot of laundry. We bought you toothbrushes and water bottles and told you to take them home.

In Conference Number Two in 2008, Saba and I became a

little more serious. The conference had a name and a program; everyone was just a little older, wiser and behaved better. The name of the conference was Art, Stamps and Chess. We learned about the handling of stamps and found the different countries that had issued them on the world globe. Saba taught those who were interested to play chess. You made an amazing copy of a beautiful painting by my friend Edna on the Venetian Masks. You made a very interesting album of wellknown paintings that you cut out of art magazines. You did a play in pantomime directed by Dotan based on my brief outline, where you included all the themes of the Conference, Art, Stamps and Chess. We were so proud of all of you.

In Conference Number 3 in 2009, Art, Music and Paris, I am sure most of you remember how we got you to see the documentary about Paris not only once but twice and how much fun we had watching it. By now, most of you have visited the city of Paris or have seen photos and films about the city. Please take out your notepads and pens and write down all the sites in Paris that you could recall.

Once everyone had finished, they watched a 3-minute film about the sites in Paris. Then we checked to see how many sites they had managed to write down. I also mentioned the play that we did and some of them began to sing the song Five People in the Family.

Yaffa (continued)

I hope you had fun with the exercise. Let us continue. **In Conference 4, 2010,** the Impressionists, remember how we had turned the living room into an art gallery and "who remembers the expensive Monet napkins?"

We then spoke about the 9 Impressionists and their beautiful paintings. Most of you remembered the painter's names. I talked about the play; mentioned the funny parts.

At this point, it was the perfect moment to distribute the beautiful, artistic folders that we had bought at the museum in Madrid. Shalom and I had also prepared baby photos, each was scanned, enlarged, and stapled onto Bristol paper. The children had to guess who was who? Of course, they were not allowed to guess their own. Everyone recognized Amit because we had to use a recent photo.

Yaffa (continued)

In Conference Number 5, 2011, Smile with Science, we were so excited when we went upstairs attired in the expensive t-shirts from San Francisco and saw the effect of the sun when the San Francisco bridge turned into color; and who can forget the experiments; the discussion around the table when you represented such important men of science.

By their smiles we knew that most of them remembered this conference well.

Conference Number 6, 2014, our last conference, A Touch of Italy Day One; Laughter Day Two". We learned the sites of Italy from the big map. You leafed through the book about Rome to see how the sites look today and how they had looked when they were constructed. Then we saw a short film about

Rome and again saw the sites how they were then and today. We learned to say a few words in Italian, prepared our 36-piece puzzle, trying to copy the beautiful magnets of the Venetian Masks. In the late afternoon, Alon and Gili joined us and we watched a film together. Then we took pajama photos and had supper together. The next day we put on a play about laughter, heard some funny jokes, played games, did artwork together and the day passed all too quickly.

Thank you for listening so quietly.

The children said that the little journey back to the six conferences brought back many memories and they rushed to look at the photo albums that I had prepared for the first four conference and first workshop and then Shani took over and did the albums for all the rest. Each family had received a copy, but they probably had not looked at them for a long time. We gave them a few minutes and then called them all back to their places so that we could continue.

Before each conference and workshop, I used to google for children jokes. For this workshop, we did something different. While in one of the bookshops in Madrid, we picked up a book of cartoons in Spanish. We made copies of some of the pages and now we passed them around the table. Each one took one page to try to decipher from the cartoon what was written in Spanish. We made extra copies so that the page could be exchanged for another one. After they tried to decipher the cartoons, I read the meaning in Spanish and translated into Hebrew. They were able to guess many meanings just by looking at the cartoons.

Following this enjoyable session, I read part 1 of my short story on Energy that I had written for my scribblers' group. I wanted the younger children not to be bored and understand some parts. The story. At first, we thought that I would read and Shalom would translate into Hebrew. But then we thought of a much better idea. Why not use one of the participants to do it in pantomime? The perfect choice was Eran, who was majoring in theatre. He sat beside me where I was standing, facing the participants and explained in pantomime the interpretation of my story. He was so good that he kept everyone laughing, not because the story was funny but because of his great gestures and wonderful acting. I want to share my story with you.

And the Lights Went Out

Yaffa Eliezer, Rehovot, October 2017

Chapter 1

Aaron was seated in front of his computer doing his assignment in English for tomorrow while at the same time giving into his new addiction "Gyro Sphere", a game on his smartphone. It was already late. His parents, sister and brother had gone to bed so that the only light in the house was the one in his room. He was doing so well that he could not stop. Suddenly the light went out and his room fell into total darkness. He took his flashlight and climbed carefully down the stairs. He tried to switch on the light in the living room and in the kitchen but there was no light. He picked up the home phone, but the line was dead.

Suddenly he felt frightened. He looked outside and saw that there was no light anywhere. He was about to go upstairs to wake up his father but then had second thoughts.

Feeling optimistic, he sat down on the couch and waited for the lights to come on. He was so tired that he lay down and fell asleep. He woke up to the early rays of dawn as the light spread into the room. He jumped up and tried the switches but there was still no power.

He rushed out the front door. He was shocked that everything had disappeared. There were no houses, no trees, no streets. Suddenly he heard a strange noise as his own house was swallowed up into the earth and disappeared in front of his eyes. The scenery began to change rapidly as the years and centuries disappeared quickly.

Suddenly he found himself on a boat out at sea. People were cramped together but he did not know anybody. Where were his parents and siblings?

He was poked by a boy twice his height who spoke to him in a strange language. He appeared angry as he punched him again. Aaron could not understand a word that he was saying. He tried to explain that he did not want to be on the boat too, but his angry neighbor became even more irritated because he did not understand a word that Aaron was saying.

The days and nights were the same. Aaron was always cold, hungry, sad and afraid. After days and nights of despair, the boat came to shore somewhere out in a deserted place with no electricity, no running water, no buildings, and almost no civilization. A small tribe of half-naked men, women and children came to greet the boat. They spoke a language that nobody on the boat understood. They shoved everybody out of the boat and onto the shore. They ripped off everyone's clothing and the new arrivals were forced to put on the local rags.

Aaron felt scared, cold and hungry. What did he do to deserve such punishment? How would he ever survive in this horrible place? All the comforts of his home were gone. He was given to eat raw food growing out of the ground and off the trees. He had to sleep on the ground. He missed his family, his bed, his mother's cooking, his computer and smart phone.

Aaron had been born into a world of high technology; a world of light; a world of cars, trains, planes, computers and smart phones. His father was a physicist working in one of the best-known laboratories in the world. He and his colleagues were doing research on fusion to solve the energy problem. The government wanted to cut down on this research because it had become too costly and the results took long in coming.

But the fuel was being used up too quickly. The world population was growing. The world needed a new source of energy, a source that would be with no pollution and available for generations to come. The pollution today from the burning of fuel and coal has resulted in environmental damage, with drastic changes in the earth's atmosphere causing disasters; scientists were warning of the consequences of the melting of the ice bergs and the rising of the waters in the oceans.

Somebody was poking him. His heart began to race. Where would they take him now? The day before he was given a spear and had to follow the group on a hunting trip. He did not know how to hunt. The locals were annoyed and refused to give him food when they returned.

Again, someone was poking him. He had to open his eyes even though he felt that his heart was about to explode out of fear.

To be continued….

It took the children a few minutes to stop laughing from Eran's pantomime. I hoped that they also understood the story.

I told them to calm down because Saba was waiting to start his talk on the workshops.

Shalom

As you know, our workshops were similar in content and level to the conferences. The only difference was that a conference lasted 2 days with a sleep over, whereas the workshops were a one-day affair. But as you may recall, every workshop had a tight schedule, keeping you busy, same as in the conferences. In the workshops we tried to learn about a variety of subjects: art and artists; science and scientists; history and geography; how people lived throughout the different periods as compared to now; the Jews in the past and today; chess, stamps etc. The idea was to accumulate knowledge with pleasure and enjoyment and to develop an imagination on subjects that most of you were not familiar with yet. It is very interesting to listen to a subject based on imagination having no knowledge of the facts.

During the workshops, we also reviewed subjects and

personalities from our previous meetings. We believe that in order to comprehend the facts, one should learn the subject many times and only then can he get a better understanding. Once you have heard this topic several times then you could learn to enjoy the subject and acquire a desire to study it in depth.

Four important things that helped with the success of all our encounters: the good food prepared by Safta; our efforts in trying to include in each meeting a variety of subjects to help you understand important and difficult topics; to have fun with art activities and entertaining short films and most important, the good atmosphere to which everyone contributed. We came away after each meeting with the impression that you were learning, creating and at the same time enjoying it all.

Now I want to take you on a journey to revisit our workshops; some visits a little more extensive than others.

The first workshop

A Day of Fun - 11.12.2007, was held a short time following our first conference. This workshop was during the Hanukkah holidays; our main discussion focused on the comparison of the living conditions during those days and today.

The second workshop

Hanukkah, – 8.12.2010, This workshop took place during the Hanukkah holiday. In this workshop each participant was supposed to create his own t-shirt by using scissors and special sewing needles that were not sharp but surprisingly most of you did not know how to thread or handle a needle. I prepared a lecture on the Jewish population of the world and used the World Map to show you where the Jewish people were scattered.

Each one of you prepared a Hanukkiah and as it was the lighting of the last candle, the 8th candle, I arranged all the Hanukkiahs together, to form one Hanukkiah and we lighted them all together.

The third workshop

Teamwork - 24.3.2012 was about communication. This workshop was very special for all of us. The preparations for this meeting were through correspondence. While we were in Madrid, Safta used the internet to communicate with you. Unlike today, not all the children had cellphones and internet connections and we needed the help of your parents to accomplish this project. It worked so well. The correspondence went back and forth. By the time we had the workshop, we all had a great time reviewing our 9 famous scientists and the 9 impressionist painters.

The fourth workshop

Fun with Cousins from Toronto in Hebrew and English, – 30.6.2012, held only 3 months later, to include our cousins' first visit from Toronto, Canada. At that time most of you did not know how to communicate in English while the Canadian cousins had either a small knowledge or none in Hebrew. We overcame this problem by doing some of the projects such as stories in the Bible, animals and so on in pantomime, just like Eran did today but of course not as professional. The explanations were in both languages.

The fifth workshop

Science and Art, - 20.3.2013, included my lecture on Scientists in the last 500 years. I asked for your participation. An interesting aspect, besides your answers to my question, was the fact that you all chose to speak about the scientist whom you had personally portrayed in Conference 5. The last part of day involved discussions around the table where you offered your opinions and the reasons why it was so important for us to continue these meetings.

The sixth workshop

Strength in Numbers, - 15.10.2014, followed two months after Conference 6, I gave a lecture on Darwin (again!) but this time it was related to the human development in big groups; the ability to communicate and collaborate in bigger numbers than other species on earth. An enjoyable activity was the play performed by you, in pantomime, written by Safta, about a family of six entitled "Six People with Only One Telephone". This was based on a true story when our children (your parents) were growing up and we had only one phone shared by six.

The seventh workshop

Person of the Century, – 28.11.2015, dealt with "Person of the Century in the last 1000 years", as chosen by the Time magazine at the end of the millennium. This Workshop involved more lectures than usual, but you were quiet, reciprocal and anxious to know; you behaved like good students. The exciting part of this project was your participation when we discussed the different aspects of these great personalities and your suggestions for those whom you favored.

When we voted for the most important personalities, including the choices from Time Magazine, it is interesting to point out that your favorites were Johann Gutenberg who invented the printing press and Albert Einstein, the great physicist of the 20th century who introduced us to his special and general relativities. Other choices were Thomas Edison the great inventor and father of the high-tech industry, Sir Isaac Newton the great physicist who found the laws of motion and of gravitation, and Christopher Columbus. The first four were suggested by Time magazine while the fifth, who discovered the Americas, was suggested by you.

The eighth workshop

Spain *and Its Jewish History – 22.10.2016*, included a general introduction to Spain, the cities where the Jewish population had lived and the influence of the Jewish culture. I began my speech with the cities that had large Jewish populations before their expulsion in 1492 from the country. I pointed out these cities on the map of Spain.

Throughout many centuries, before their expulsions, the

Jews in Spain were the largest and most prosperous Jewish community in the world. The Spanish Jews were the leaders of the World Jewry in philosophical studies and in literature, including Hebrew poetry, for the first time since the period of the Bible. A few important Jewish personalities with great achievements were described. I then discussed them with you.

The highlight of this conference was around the table discussion. I asked you how you had enjoyed this conference with the combination of so many lectures and short films. Almost everyone came to the same conclusion that the break in the lectures with a short film helps you understand and appreciate the lecture better.

<u>The ninth workshop</u>

Fun with Cousins from Toronto in English, – 1.1.2017. By now all of you understood and spoke English, some better than others, and the Canadian cousins knew a little bit of Hebrew. Communication was not a problem. The main lectures were on geography subjects with emphasis on the flags of various nations. You all received white t-shirts and had to create your own design with special markers. This workshop took place one day after Hanukkah, so I gave a talk about the historical perspective of this holiday.

Today we have our, workshop 10, We Did It Our Way. I hope that you will enjoy this workshop. We tried very hard to maintain the standards of our previous workshops, while taking into consideration the gap in ages. We made some special efforts to make it understandable to all whenever possible. Thank you for listening so quietly.

By the time Shalom finished his talk, the children were starving. Some of the participants helped me set up the table for lunch.

Afterwards, when the tables were cleared again, I brought a huge zippered up shopping bag and told the children that inside was a new game. It went from hand to hand while they tried to guess what type of game was inside, but it was too difficult. Inside the bag was a set of 52 playing cards and 2 jokers, each one the size of a placemat. As soon as they saw the cards, they all became excited. The first question that Alon asked was if the cards were one of the items for the Bazaar. He was very disappointed when I said no.

How did I come across these cards? It helps if you find yourself at the right place, at the right time. While on our last visit to Montreal, we went up north for the day with my cousin and his wife. As we were strolling down one of the streets, my eyes caught sight of a small shop for kitchen accessories. I love shopping for kitchen gadgets and of course we went inside; and behold among all the kitchen treasures was a display of huge playing cards. They were the size of regular placemats; I knew right away that I had to buy them.

Now to get back to our card game. Here too I spent several hours making up two novel card games. In the end we had time only for one. These games should be played by up to four players but since we had many more, each participant received only 4 cards and thus there were only four cards left in the deck.

·   ·   ·

The Card Game:

*order of the cards: like in the well-known card game Bridge, the 4 suits are called **spades, hearts, diamonds, and clubs.** The numbers are from 2 to 10 followed by the jack, the queen, the king and the ace. Before the cards are dealt, the person who receives the first card, is the one who cuts the cards and places this card upside down. This card is the trump. After all the cards are dealt, the person who was dealt first, plays a card of his choice. If the other players have neither the same number, nor the same suit nor a trump card, they can get rid of a card of their choice. When two or more of the same number are thrown, a war is declared. Each player puts one card upside down and one open and the highest card is the winner except for the trump that takes all.*

Back to the game

As there are only 52 cards in the stack, each participant received only 4 cards. The cards were so big to hold that most of them had to put them upside down on the table.

The first player opened his card. Every player followed with a card of the same suit or with a trump card. After each round there remained less and less players. The tension was felt when only two players were left. And then we had a winner and the game was over.

The participants were very excited and wanted to try the second game that I had prepared but since the first one took so long, we did not continue with the cards.

Following this exciting card game, I read part 2 of my story on energy and again Eran kept everyone laughing. I do not know how much they understood, but for the benefit of Alon and Gili it was a wise choice to have him do the pantomime.

And the Lights Went Out

Chapter 2

Aaron woke up. He smiled as he looked up into his father's blue eyes. He was so relieved to see him that he wrapped his hands around his neck and held on tightly.

"Aaron you're choking me. Are you okay? Are you sick? Why are you sleeping on the coach?"

"The light went out in my room after you all fell asleep. I came downstairs and the power was down in the entire house. I lay down on the couch and I must have fallen asleep."

"The power is back; go upstairs and get ready for school."

"I had a horrible dream. It was the worst dream that I ever had. First, I was on a boat, then I was taken to a primitive place where there was no electricity, no running water; it was like going back in time hundreds of years ago. I was alone, hungry, cold and scared."

"Aaron calm down. You are trembling. It was only a dream."

"It was a nightmare! If we won't have electricity everything will change."

"Aaron, it was only a small power failure."

"Promise me that we will always have electricity in America."

"Don't worry. The world still has raw materials to last a long time. There are many resources available today. There are also new ideas in the process of research. You do not have to worry. Now go get dressed or you'll be late for school."

Aaron was very quiet all day. During recess he refused to play with his classmates. He could not stop thinking about the horrible dream.

As soon as he returned home, he searched Google about the ongoing research on energy. He read that at present most of the world consumption of energy comes from the oil reserves, natural gas, coal, solar and wind. The solar and wind systems are still not economically viable and not in abundance. Today the cheapest sources of energy are still oil and coal. But these two sources are causing environmental damage and the pollution is spreading. Global warming is growing. He was surprised to learn that the European Union had decided that in the future cars that run on gasoline will be banned. Even today there are already electrical cars used in some parts of the world.

What could he do to help? He was ready to stop playing his games on the cell phone all the time, use the air conditioner less, use his bike more and walk instead of asking his mother to take him by car everywhere. He was ready to do anything that his father will recommend, well, almost anything. Maybe if he did his part, the horrible dream would not return.

Suddenly an idea came to his head. Well, two ideas but one step at a time. He was sure that his teacher would approve. Already he felt better. He was doing something; maybe it was not much but still it was a start.

He was so busy that his mother had to call him several times before he finally came down to the dining room.

"Aaron, how many times do I have to call you? Were you playing that stupid game Gyro Sphere on your phone?"

"No, Mom. I swear. I was preparing something for class."

"Did you get an assignment in English?"

"No, it's not for English. This is for my Physics class. It is not an assignment. It is something that… I can't tell you about it now, maybe tomorrow. Where is Dad?"

"You didn't get an assignment and you are preparing something for your Physics class? Aaron, are you feeling okay."

"I'm fine Mom. Where is Dad?"

"He has to work late tonight. You better finish your supper and go to sleep. I heard that you slept on the couch last night and had a bad dream."

"It was so horrible, but I don't want to talk about it now." To be continued…

Because of Eran's wonderful acting, my story went over much better than I had originally anticipated. Sometimes the scene was difficult but even when he just sat there shaking his head, he was funny. It had kept everyone in his seat and in a very good mood especially when they knew that next on the program was the Bazaar!

At first Shalom and I discussed the idea of giving them real money but due to the unsuccessful experience in Workshop 7, we decided to use the monopoly money again. This time the bazaar included: a food market, the big games that were gathering dust that included the big chess set, the huge O X game and the rope game. We also put out many games from our cupboard and a few newly bought high quality coloring pencils, expensive notebooks, etc...

The food section included a good bottle of red wine, one of olive oil, a good blend of ground black coffee, some boxes of wafers, chocolates, bagel, sweets etc. The siblings joined forces for the big items and sometimes the bidding was so high that they had little money left for the small items that the younger participants wanted. But at the end there was nothing left; they had spent all their money, and everyone was happy.

I read the third and last part of my story as soon as everyone was seated and Eran was beside me.

And the Lights Went Out

Chapter 3

As soon as he came to school, Aaron went to look for his Physics teacher, Mr. Sander. He found him in the teacher's room. Mr. Sander was surprised to see Aaron, one of his less enthusiastic students of physics. When Aaron showed him his presentation that he had prepared, he was not only surprised but delighted and agreed to let Aaron present it to the class.

Aaron could not concentrate on the studies during the entire morning. His mind was on his presentation. He waited anxiously; it was the first time that he was so anxious and excited before the Physics class. Finally, the bell chimed for recess. His friends asked him to play but he declined. At last the recess ended and the students returned to class.

Mr. Sanders addressed the class and told them that he had

received an unexpected request from Aaron to present a talk on the topic of Energy. He asked everyone to cooperate. A few sighs escaped from some of his classmates. Aaron ignored them and showed his first slide entitled ENERGY with the following verse that he had composed.

Energy is responsible for our "easy life."

Without energy, civilization cannot survive.

Energy provides light and heat.

It enables man to grow his food so that he could eat.

He then turned to his classmates and began his lecture.

I do not know how many of you realize what will happen when we have used up all our sources of energy. What happens when we have no energy? I know that you do not care and haven't even thought about it. Truthfully, neither did I until two days ago when we had a small blackout in our residential area. All the power was down. The entire house was in total darkness. Everyone in my house was asleep. I was alone in the dark with no light and no heat. I was lucky that I had my flashlight. I went downstairs to check if we had light anywhere in the house and I fell asleep. I had the most horrible dream that scared me to death. It is for this reason that I have prepared a few questions. I hope that they will enable all of us to understand how important it is for us to have energy.

1. What is energy?
2. How do we get energy today?
3. How would you rate the sources of energy?
4. How would you imagine life today without energy?

Mr. Sanders gave each student a sheet of paper to write down his answers.

"Is this an exam? It is not fair. We just had one two days ago."

"No, it's not an exam, just a small survey that Aaron has prepared."

"Are we going to get marks for it?"

The teacher became angry. This is the only thing that interested most of the students today, marks.

"I have not decided yet. It all depends on your cooperation and your answers."

"Can we use Google?"

"No, I want to see what you know not what Google knows. Please put your smartphones away. Whoever uses his phone will be disqualified."

The children reluctantly put their phones away. They had no choice but to use their heads and think. The teacher was already pleased.

They tried to recall what they had learned in school, at home or from the TV. Some of the replies were childish and baseless. Following are a glimpse into the more intelligent ones.

Question Number 1: What is energy?

Anything that will cause something else to move is energy.

If there is no energy you cannot do anything.

Electricity is a source of energy.

Energy is what makes people do negative and positive things.

Question No. 2: How do we get energy today?

Today we get energy from oil, gas, coal, solar, hydro, geothermal, biomass, and wind.

Question No. 3: How would you rate the different sources of energy that are used today?

The solar is too expensive. Carbon causes too much pollution; in nuclear energy there is a danger of explosion.

Question No. 4: How would you imagine life without energy?

Without energy life today would be very boring, no smartphones, no computers, no television.

I would not know what to do.

With no energy the world population will starve.

We must not allow a situation where the energy will become deplete.

It was amazing how quickly the physics class had passed. The teacher collected the children's replies and turned to Aaron.

"You did a great job. I hope to see you as a more enthusiastic and participating student in my class from now on."

"You bet."

"Any more plans?"

"I definitely will take more interest in the physics class."

"Are you planning to prepare another presentation?"

"No, I have a better idea. I will ask my father to present a lecture on energy to the class. He's an amazing lecturer."

"That is a great idea!"

Before Shalom's lecture, we took time out for the bathroom, stretch our legs, have a quick snack and everyone was back in the living room.

Shalom

<u>The Good the Bad and the Ugly</u>

My talk now is a popular scientific lecture on the energy problem. I will also describe in brief my scientific involvement in future fusion energy production. The title of this talk characterizes energy as "the Good, the Bad and the Ugly." I borrowed this title from the 1966 Italian American famous western film, directed by Sergio Leone and starring Clint Eastwood as the "good guy," Lee Van Cleef as the "bad guy" and Eli Wallach as the "ugly guy."

All of you remember Charles Darwin and his theory that all species and humans were developed from a common ancestor. On the historical route to survival, the ones who won, were the fittest on our planet. I would like to add to this picture the attributed saying by the famous scientist Ludwig Boltzmann who in 1886 said that "the struggle for existence is the struggle for available energy."

Without energy our civilization cannot survive. What can be bad in energy? Isn't energy always good? The answer is NO! Energy can also heat up our planet and change our climate causing severe damages. Before classifying the different energies, I would like to present some numbers (in percentage) on the global electricity production in the year 2017. This energy from coal is 38%, from oil 3% (the energy consumed by cars is not included here) and from gas 23%. These fossil fuels pollute the atmosphere and are the main reason for the quick heating of our planet; they are therefore classified as the bad. Not all the fossil fuels are bad on the same level. The coal is much more polluting than the gas, still all fossils are polluting and are bad. Ten percent of the total energy is nuclear fission energy that I refer to as "ugly". Why ugly if it does not pollute the atmosphere? This energy is obtained by splitting heavy nuclei, such as uranium. During this process one can have an accident such as the one that occurred in Chernobyl, the then Soviet Union (and today Ukraine) in 1986. The nuclear reactors have "leftovers" that must be safely kept for thousands of years.

So, who are the good guys? The ones that do not pollute the atmosphere and are not causing large damages and disasters. Continuing now with the good numbers, we have 16% of electricity produced by waterfalls (hydropower) and 10% is solar, wind, biomass and geothermal.

Following is my diagram of the good, the bad and the ugly.

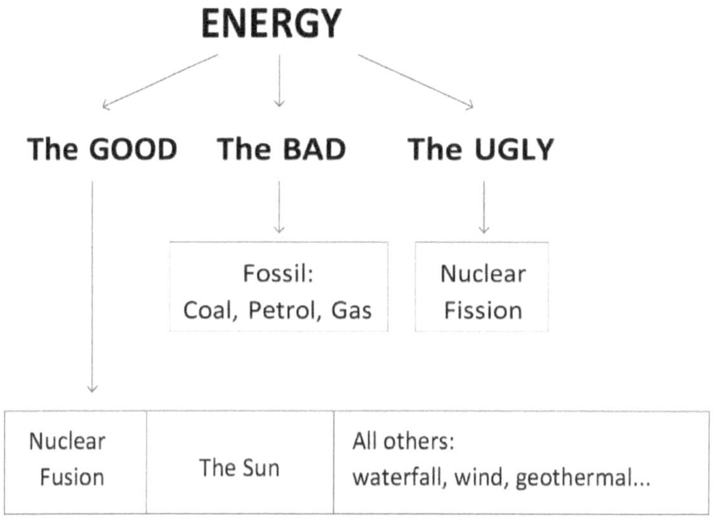

For the future, we need the good energy to be the most used for consumption. Can we increase the 26% used today to 90% to produce electricity? It looks almost impossible, yet scientists have suggested a novel energy produced by nuclear fusion that does not pollute and no disasters are intrinsically possible."

What is fusion and how can we achieve it?

"As you know all matter is composed of atoms. An atom has electrons moving around the nucleus at its center. Whoever learned about the Mendeleev table of the atoms knows that at the beginning of the table there are the light elements (atoms) such as hydrogen and helium, and at the end of this table we have the heavy elements such as uranium.

In the **fission reactor,** the nucleus of the heavy atom is split into smaller pieces; some mass is lost during this process which is converted into energy. Today about 10% of the electric energy consumption comes from this process. This energy is clean, namely it does not pollute the atmosphere; but I did not classify it in the good category because it is possible to have a disastrous accident. Even without accidents, the leftovers in a fission reactor are radioactive and must be hidden safely for a few tens of thousands of years. Remember that our civilization is only 10,000 years old.

In the **fusion reactor** the nuclei of the light elements are used to combine and when they fuse together, part of the mass is lost; this energy is released again according to the Einstein equation. To understand this Einstein mass to energy conversion, it is useful to know that one kilogram (kg) of nuclear fuel of fusion is equivalent to the burning of 10 million kg of coal! Our sun is such a nuclear fusion reactor. This means that instead of burning 10,000,000 kg of coal we should use one kilogram of "good fuel" (such as heavy hydrogen) and get the same energy without pollution or accidents!

The fusion reactions in our sun create the energy that supply the light and the heat that we receive on our planet for our existence. The origin of this energy in our Sun (like in our universe) is nuclear fusion energy.

Can we produce this type of energy in the laboratory? Why don't we have such fusion reactors yet? What are the problems? The center of the sun, where the nuclear fusion energy is produced, is extremely hot. No material on earth can sustain such temperatures. However, 58 years ago, after the laser was invented, (by Theodore Maiman in 1960) scientists in the USA and independently in the Soviet Union, suggested to use the lasers on a small scale to heat the heavy hydrogen. In our oceans, there is one molecule with heavy hydrogen for every 6000 water molecules in the oceans. Thus, the fuel supply for fusion is practically unlimited for energy purposes. In this case scientists suggested that the walls of the reactor chamber be built many meters away from the center so that the extremely hot center cannot damage the chamber while at the same time releasing the fusion energy.

Today we can create this small sun in many laboratories around the world, including Israel, but we are not efficient enough to get a gain of energy. In different parts of the world, scientists including myself, are working on this subject. This approach is called inertial confinement fusion (ICF) and the scientists in many countries expect to have such power reactors ready in about 20 years, for experimental proof.

The laser created small sun is not the only scheme used to produce fusion energy in a reactor on our planet. About 20 years before the laser was invented, scientists suggested to confine very dilute (densities less than 100,000 times in the air in the room) plasmas of the heavy hydrogen atoms. The idea is to heat this plasma to high enough temperatures and to confine the electrically charged particles (the electrons and the nuclei) by magnetic fields. This approach is called magnetic confinement fusion (MCF). An international MCF collaboration called ITER (International Experimental Reactor) is being built. It is a 500-megawatt power reactor in the Cadarache facility in Saint-Paul-les Durance, in the Provence in southern France. This will be the largest nuclear fusion magnetic plasma confinement reactor that is foreseen to operate by 2025.

Thank you for your patience. I hope I did not bore you. I know that this is not an easy subject.

Following Shalom's lecture, came the part of the program that everyone looked forward to "the souvenirs". This time the participants received the following:

Their old toothbrushes and new ones

Their old water bottles and new ones (the same as the one that Amit had received)

A new post it package

A new generation disk on key that already contained copies of the musical presentations that Shani had prepared; one of the first four conferences and one workshop and the other, a new one, with Conferences 5 and 6 and Workshops 2 to 9. On the disc Shani also copied for them the play from Conference 3, the play from Conference 4, the discussion of the scientists from Conference 5, the play about laughter from Conference 6 and a short film of Kofiko- the monkey, which was the children's favorite when they were small.

The girls received smart looking bags with a bottle of perfume inside

The boys back packs with cologne bottles inside

Gili and Alon received special backpacks with very small bottles of perfume/cologne and pencil cases with sharpeners and lots of chocolates.

At the end of the workshop, three participants got together and performed the texts of **The Four States of Matter** in English and Hebrew to rap music. Dotan did the first verse in English, then Tamir and Eran did the second and third verses in Hebrew. All the other participants sat in the living room, clapping their hands in tune to the Rap, sometimes some high-pitched notes were heard.

Following their hard work, they all went into the Grandchildren Room while Shalom and I prepared the table for supper that we were going to have together with their parents.

When the table was all set, we put four containers in the center, each one representing a number, and all together formed the year 2019. I filled these with goodies. The table looked very festive.

Once all the parents arrived, the participants joined them and told them about the great day that we all had.

Following supper, the parents wanted the children to perform the Rap song, but they were too tired. I promised to mail it to them so that they could see the clip quietly in their free time.

The grownups gathered around in the living room to see the two musical presentations that Shani had prepared for all the conferences and workshops. They also saw two of the plays that we had staged in Conference 3 and Conference 4. They were excited to see the big change in their children too.

Before they left, some of the children said that this was the best workshop so far. Dotan told Shalom that he enjoyed his lecture on The Good, The Bad and the Ugly and would be very happy to hear another scientific lecture soon.

The house was again quiet. We were tired and happy.

EPILOGUE

Thirteen years ago, my husband and I initiated a project with nine of our grandchildren, ages 3 to 9. It all began as a pajama party that quickly turned into a traditional affair coined by Shalom "Grandchildren Conference."

Why did we bother to hold these unique get-togethers? The children loved these meetings of learning while having fun. The big rewards were to hear the exciting voices on the phone when a new theme was introduced in school that was already familiar to them and they could proudly participate.

Children are very smart; they are like sponges. They are ready to learn new things when they are given the proper surroundings and attention because they are hungry for knowledge. When it is handed out in an appetizing surrounding with fun, they learn quickly. We wanted to introduce them to the past, the present and the future developments.

When I first came up with the idea of the pajama party,

never in my wildest dreams did I imagine that it would lead in the direction that it has. It has been a lot of hard work. We are both happy that we were able to do this project. We enjoyed preparing the themes; they had fun learning them.

Why did we continue with this project? Once we began, it became as important to us as much as to the children. We enjoyed seeing them maturing and asking clever question as the material became more difficult. It bonded the cousins together and it bonded us to them.

Who could have imagined that our first conference that began as a pajama party would lead to Workshop 10 with a lecture on the energy problem and a rap song on the four states of matter?

What began as a one-time affair led to six Grandchildren Conferences and ten Workshops that are unforgettable to all of us.